WHY CHURCH?

DISCOVER 12 LIFE-CHANGING BENEFITS FOR YOU

BY BOB HOSTETLER

Published by Outreach, Inc. Colorado Springs, CO 80919
www.Outreach.com
All Scripture quotations, unless otherwise indicated, are taken from the Holy Bible, New International Version®, NIV®, Copyright © 1973, 1978, 1984, 2011 by Biblica. Used by permission of Zondervan Publishing House. All rights reserved worldwide.

Some Scripture quotations are taken from the Contemporary English Version (CEV) ®, Copyright © 1995 American Bible Society. All rights reserved.

Some Scripture quotations are taken from the King James Version (KJV).

Some Scripture quotations are taken from the Holy Bible, New Living Translation (NLT), copyright © 1996, 2004, 2007 by Tyndale House Foundation. Used by permission of Tyndale House Publishers, Inc., Carol Stream, Illinois 60188. All rights reserved.

Some Scripture quotations are taken from the New American Standard Bible® (NASB), Copyright © 1960, 1962, 1963, 1968, 1971, 1972, 1973, 1975, 1977, 1995 by The Lockman Foundation. Used by permission.

Some Scripture quotations are taken from the New Century Version of the Bible (NCV) , copyright © 2005 by Thomas Nelson, Inc. Used by permission.

Some Scripture quotations are taken from The Message (MSG), Copyright © by Eugene H. Peterson 1993, 1994, 1995, 1996, 2000, 2001, 2002. Used by permission of NavPress Publishing Group.

Some Scripture quotations are taken from The Holy Bible, English Standard Version® (ESV®), copyright © 2001 by Crossway, a publishing ministry of Good News Publishers. Used by permission.

Some Scripture quotations are taken from the Good News Translation® (GNT) (Today's English Version, Second Edition), Copyright © 1992 American Bible Society. All rights reserved.

Some Scripture quotations are taken from New Revised Standard Version of the Bible (NRSV), copyright © 1946, 1952, and 1971 National Council of the Churches of Christ in the United States of America. Used by permission. All rights reserved.

Some Scripture quotations are taken from the Holy Bible, New International Reader's Version®, NIrV® Copyright © 1995, 1996, 1998 by Biblica, Inc.™ Used by permission of Zondervan. All rights reserved worldwide. www.zondervan.com The "NIrV" and "New International Reader's Version" are trademarks registered in the United States Patent and Trademark Office by Biblica, Inc.™

ISBN: 978-1-935541-70-7

Written by: Bob Hostetler
Cover Design: Tim Downs
Interior Design: Tim Downs
Printed in the United States of America

CONTENTS

INTRODUCTION

Church steeples don't dominate the landscape as they once did, but you still see church buildings nearly everywhere. Some are empty. Others have been converted to private homes, upscale restaurants, or craft stores. But many still operate as churches. The signs out front advertise Sunday school and worship services, and sometimes a weeknight service or prayer meeting.

And, apparently, people still attend these churches. You see cars in the parking lot on Sundays when you're not sleeping in or out on the lake. Some are obviously larger than others, and some appear more traditional while others hardly look like churches at all.

That's fine for some people, but not everyone. Maybe not you.

Some people were raised by churchgoing parents. They were required to dress up and attend church every Sunday. They squirmed through stuffy sanctuaries and interminable sermons as children, and eventually, when they grew up and were able to choose, they saw no point in going to church. It was boring. It seemed pointless. It added nothing to their lives.

Other people once attended church regularly, even enthusiastically, but stopped. Maybe they left home (and church) for college and never looked back. Or they may have married, started a career, had children, and just got too busy for church. Others became disillusioned, moved to a new community, or started questioning their faith. Some could probably cite "all the above" as reasons they no longer associate with a church.

And, of course, a great many people never began attending church and have never seen a reason to start. Their lives are quite full. They have families and friends. They have demanding jobs and packed calendars. They may enter a church building for weddings or funerals from time to time, but otherwise they never feel drawn to religious observances. Many of these people have faith. Many long for more, spiritually speaking. But they don't see a Christian church as having anything to offer them.

All sorts of people could reasonably ask the question, "Who needs the church these days?"

WHY CHURCH?

It is a valid question. There are lots of reasons that "going to church" seems outdated and irrelevant to many people today. To many, churches largely belong to a bygone age of men wearing ties, women in white gloves, and cars with fins. Some churches seem woefully out-of-touch with today's increasingly fast-paced, technology-driven, skeptically minded world. And, judging from much of what appears on Christian television, churches don't have much to offer in this day and age.

"I work long hours at least six days a week," says Tom, a forty-seven-year-old executive. "'Church' doesn't even appear on my radar. What little time I have leftover at the end of my workweek, I focus on my wife and stepchildren. There's just no room for anything else."

Elyse is a thirty-two-year-old mother and economics professor. "When we first moved to this community [the college town where she teaches], my husband and I actually checked out a few churches, but we quickly gave up. We couldn't find one that was a 'fit' for our family."

"I swore I'd never go back," says Andrea, a single mom who went through a nasty divorce seven years ago. "When my husband walked out on us, our church didn't know how to respond. They mostly ignored me and my [nine-year-old] daughter. We were both confused and hurting, and no one seemed to know what to say to us, other than 'we'll pray for you.' We needed so much more than that, and no one seemed to care."

No wonder so many people have given up on the church. No wonder it seems irrelevant to some. There are so many different kinds of churches, and so many different kinds of people in them. Churches have long given off a distinct aura, and it's not always a positive one. Churches can be stuck in the past. They seem to be "against" things more than they are "for" things. Their views on sexuality and science seem outdated. They seem to be largely out of touch with what most people are interested in and what people are looking for these days.

Those are sweeping generalizations, of course. But they are not completely detached from reality. Many churches have been slow to innovate (though some people find solace in meaningful traditions and rituals). Many churches have struggled to keep up with our rapidly changing culture, but then, so have many individuals and other institutions. Many churches have expended more energy defending the status quo than effectively translating timeless truths in a way that meets people's needs today, although you may be surprised at how God still manages to do amazing things in people's lives in spite of the church's shortcomings.

Churches today are as varied—and as flawed—as the people who inhabit them. Not one of them is perfect, of course. But believe it or not, every one of them has value. Every Christ-centered church has a role to play and a divine purpose to fulfill.

WHOSE IDEA WAS IT, ANYWAY?

Many years ago, an ancient scribe recorded a poetic account of the earth's origins. He wrote that in the very beginning of things, "God said, 'Let there be light,' and there was light."[1] He described the appearance of the sun and moon, stars and planets, oceans and dry land, plants and animals, fish and birds.

And after each burst of creative activity, that ancient chronicler depicted God's reaction: "It was good."[2]

God creates good things: snowflakes, sunshine, rose petals, peaches, mountain streams, seasons, golden retrievers, eagles, color, taste, hummingbirds, the Himalayas, the Great Barrier Reef...even people.

Among the good things God created is the church, if you can believe it. It was His idea. It was His doing. The Bible records how it happened:

> After [Jesus'] death, he presented himself alive to [his followers] in many different settings over a period of forty days. In face-to-face meetings, he talked to them about things concerning the kingdom of God. As they met and ate meals together, he told them that they were on no account to leave Jerusalem but "must wait for what the Father promised: the promise you heard from me. John baptized in water; you will be baptized in the Holy Spirit. And soon."...
>
> When the Feast of Pentecost came, they were all together in one place. Without warning there was a sound like a strong wind, gale force—no one could tell where it came from. It filled the whole building. Then, like a wildfire, the Holy Spirit spread through their ranks, and they started speaking in a number of different languages as the Spirit prompted them."[3]

Well, because the Feast of Pentecost was one of the major events in the calendar for Jews around the civilized world at that time, tens of thousands of people were visiting Jerusalem and making their way to the temple on that very day. And the building where Jesus' followers had gathered sat on a major thoroughfare through the city. So when that group tumbled out of the second-floor room where they had been meeting and took up posts along the street, travelers and tourists not only stopped but flocked to the spot, because in the midst of all the Aramaic-shouting shopkeepers and hawkers along the street, they suddenly heard their native languages being spoken.

But as the size of the crowd increased, so did people's confusion. Because what they discovered was not other people from Mesopotamia or Phrygia, Egypt or Libya or Rome; they saw a group of country preachers—apparently from Galilee—who somehow seemed to be speaking in whatever language the hearers could understand! It was baffling. What they saw and what they were hearing didn't line up. And most disorienting of all, it seemed that a person from Persia and another from Rome could be standing side by side, listening to one of those people speak, and yet each one understood the speaker perfectly.

Finally, one of the Galileans by the name of Peter called for everyone's attention and started addressing the whole crowd, which had swelled to thousands of people. He answered the suggestion of some in the crowd who thought alcohol had to be involved in some way. He said that he and the others were not under the influence of alcohol, but that they were under the influence of God's Spirit. He said they were all witnessing something the prophet Joel had promised centuries before:

> "In the Last Days," God says,
> "I will pour out my Spirit
>   on every kind of people:
> Your sons will prophesy,
>   also your daughters;
> Your young men will see visions,
>   your old men dream dreams....
> And whoever calls out for help
>   to me, God, will be saved."[4]

Peter went on to explain that all this was happening because of Jesus, the Galilean miracle-worker everyone had heard about, who had been arrested and executed not long ago, right there in Jerusalem. "But," the man named Peter said, "God untied the death ropes and raised him up. Death was no match for him.... And every one of us here is a witness to it. Then, raised to the heights at the right hand of God and receiving the promise of the Holy Spirit from the Father, he poured out the Spirit he had just received. That is what you see and hear."

Suddenly, someone at the front shouted, "Now what do we do?" Others echoed the question, and soon Peter motioned for quiet.

He answered, "Change your life. Turn to God and be baptized, each of you, in the name of Jesus Christ, so your sins are forgiven. Receive the gift of the Holy Spirit. The promise is targeted to you and your children, but also to all who are far away—whomever, in fact, our Master God invites."[5]

That day, three thousand of those visitors to Jerusalem from all over the world responded to the message and were baptized. They became followers of Jesus, the risen Messiah, and charter members of the first church in history.

That was a few years ago, of course (nearly two thousand years, in fact), and a lot has changed since then. But the church that exists today is the same organism God created less than two months after Jesus was crucified, buried, and rose from the dead. In some places, it may seem outdated or irrelevant, but it exists around the world and speaks hundreds of languages. To some people, it may not seem all that appealing or applicable to life in the twenty-first century, but it was God's idea. The church is crucial to God's hopes and dreams for people to this day.

NOW MORE THAN EVER

For all its flaws and shortcomings, the church is more important today. As hard as it may be to believe right now, the church is needed more in the twenty-first century than ever before. Wherever you are in your spiritual journey, "church" has more to offer you and your family than you can imagine...right now.

We live in a day and age in which so much is changing quickly. Technology is transforming our lives in a multitude of ways—some good, some bad, but often in disconcerting and disorienting ways. Stresses and strains on individuals, marriages, and families have never been so pronounced. The once-supportive structures of schools, neighborhoods, and community associations have lost the authority and ability to honor our values and ideals (and it sometimes seems like they work against them). Even the brightest and most conscientious people among us have pressing questions and needs that no one seems equipped to answer. Modern people have a plethora of deeply and widely felt needs that can be met in a Bible-teaching church of virtually any shape and size. A need to ask questions and seek answers; to have an anchor, a center, a point of reference in life; to figure some things out and gain a new perspective from time to time; to fit in, to belong, to forge some kind of community; to feel alive and more intimately connected with God; to learn and grow and feel like they are going somewhere; to feel useful and pursue what matters; to rest and heal; to express what is inside them; and more.

Those are the things this book will address. Each one is an answer to the question, "Why Church?" Each one is intensely practical, hugely important, and utterly applicable to your life now—today.

"AFTER ALL THESE YEARS, I AM STILL INVOLVED IN THE PROCESS OF SELF-DISCOVERY. IT'S BETTER TO EXPLORE LIFE AND MAKE MISTAKES THAN TO PLAY IT SAFE."
—SOPHIA LOREN

CHAPTER 1

EXPLORE

Entering a church for the first time can be a little scary. You had no trouble finding a parking place. You lock your car and head for the entrance. Just inside the double doors, some guy with a handful of paper programs thrusts his hand your direction, and says, "Good morning."

You had wanted your entrance to be unnoticed, but after you shake his hand, he hands you a program and turns away to welcome the next person. You look around the lobby and spy the doors to the auditorium. You duck in quickly and take your seat in the back. A few people smile and say hello before the music starts. You make a mental note to dash out as soon as the service ends.

That may not describe your first time attending a church service, but it fits many people's experience. Like most new things, entering a church for the first time can be slightly nerve-racking, which is why some people choose never to darken the doors of a church. They're not sure how to dress. They're afraid they might be singled out. They worry they might do something wrong, something embarrassing.

It shouldn't be that way, of course, but it is. Not necessarily because we are shy or insecure; and not necessarily because churches aren't sufficiently welcoming or open to first-time visitors. In some cases, it's just that "church" is a new experience. It is *terra incognita,* uncharted territory, and only the most adventurous types of people like to enter such places.

Nearly all of us, however, would like to find a safe place where we can ask questions and seek answers. After all, you sense that you're on some sort of journey, and though you may be at a different place than others around you—and you may be traveling at a different pace—you wouldn't mind a little help along the way. You wouldn't mind being able to explore things like God, Jesus, and the Bible, without being judged or made to feel stupid. But you're not sure you can realistically expect that from the church.

Church Is a Place for All Kinds of People

From the very beginning, the church has been a place for all kinds of people. As described in the introduction, the church was born on a Sunday in Jerusalem, when thousands of Jews from around the world gathered for one of the major yearly festivals (called Pentecost or the Feast of Weeks). That was the occasion God chose to send His Holy Spirit to fill Jesus' first followers and enable them to speak to people from every corner of the earth in their own languages: "Parthians and Medes and Elamites and residents of Mesopotamia, Judea and Cappadocia, Pontus and Asia, Phrygia and Pamphylia, Egypt and the parts of Libya belonging to Cyrene, and visitors from Rome, both Jews and proselytes, Cretans and Arabians."[1] With one miraculous and dramatic action, God made it clear that this new thing we now call "the church" was intended to include all kinds of people.

And that was only the beginning. A few years later, Philip, another of Jesus' earliest followers, went to an area called Samaria to tell people about Jesus. The people of that area were so despised by people of Jewish descent that a sort of apartheid existed between Jews and Samaritans. Yet, when Philip reported to the rest of the church's leadership in Jerusalem that the Samaritans had reacted warmly to his preaching, "They sent to them Peter and John, who came down and prayed for them that they might receive the Holy Spirit....Then they laid their hands on them and they received the Holy Spirit."[2] In other words, God followed up the *Jewish* Pentecost with a *Samaritan* Pentecost, which ought to show us how accepting God intended the church to be.

But that's still not all. Just a few years after the Samaritans received God's Holy Spirit (thus becoming part of the church), the same Peter—who had delivered the main sermon in Jerusalem on the Day of Pentecost and traveled with John to Samaria for the Samaritan Pentecost—was invited to the home of a Roman centurion in a town called Caesarea. In those days it was unacceptable for a Jew (which Peter was, ethnically and culturally speaking) to enter the home of a Gentile, let alone that of an officer in the hated armies of Caesar. But just the night before, God spoke to Peter in a vision, and told him that he was no longer to consider any person "unclean." So he went to the home of that centurion, whose name was Cornelius, and began to tell him, his family, and his friends about Jesus. Before Peter even finished speaking, "the Holy Spirit fell upon all who were listening to the message. The Jewish believers who came with Peter were amazed that the gift of the Holy Spirit had been poured out on the Gentiles, too."[3] A third "Pentecost" had taken place, making it clear that even people with no Jewish blood or background were to be included in this new thing we now call "the church."

It was God's intention from the very beginning for "church" to be a place—a group, a gathering—for all kinds of people. Although churches have often strayed from that ideal through the centuries, it remains God's intention today.

Church Is a Place to Ask Questions

The book of Acts, the fifth book of the New Testament, tells the story of the church's birth and development in the first three decades after Jesus' death, resurrection, and ascension. You will hear more about this fascinating book of the Bible in the chapters to come.

If you were to survey every chapter in that story of the early church, you would discover more than fifty questions people asked. Some of those questions are investigative: "How can this be?"[4] and "What can this mean?"[5] Some are rhetorical: "Why does it seem incredible to any of you that God can raise the dead?"[6] Some are probing: "Do you want to know how he was healed?"[7] and "Do you understand what you are reading?"[8] Some are intended to correct: "Friends, why are you doing this?"[9] And others reflect sincere searching: "What must I do to be saved?"[10] and "What prevents me from being baptized?"[11]

Too often, people in the church feel like they have to have all the answers. But that wasn't true in the early church, and it doesn't have to be true today, either. Pastors and teachers in the church may have some answers to some really important questions, but churches that are most like the early church are a great place for people's questions.

Author David Kinnaman writes,

> God is not afraid of human doubts. "Doubting Thomas" is remembered for his unbelief, yet in his mercy, Christ allowed Thomas to renew his faith when the risen Lord displayed the evidence of his crucifixion and resurrection. King David is called a man after God's heart, even though many of his psalms questioned God's intentions toward and provision for him—many times in raw, angry language that leaves very little emotion unexpressed. Job too voiced his doubts and disillusionment in very strong terms.[12]

A church community can provide a great opportunity to ask sincere, searching questions. It can be a safe place to voice your doubts, just like the early church. Good questions and hard questions, like those asked by Thomas, David, and Job. Probing questions and open-ended questions. Such as, "How can this be?" and "What can this mean?" Or, "How was he healed?" and "Why are you doing this?" And, "What must I do to be saved?" and "What prevents me from being baptized?"

Church Is a Place for People on a Journey

The book of Acts relates a fascinating incident in the early days of the church. Philip, one of Jesus' first followers, met an Ethiopian man on a desert road between Jerusalem and Gaza. The traveler, a high official in the court of the Ethiopian queen, had made a pilgrimage to worship at the temple in Jerusalem, and was on the return trip.

Philip, under the guidance of God's Holy Spirit, approached

the regal chariot and saw a scroll open on the man's lap. The Ethiopian may have worn a puzzled expression or been shaking his head, which prompted Philip to ask, "Do you understand what you're reading?"

The man wasn't insulted or embarrassed. He answered, "I don't see how I can, without someone who can explain it to me." He invited Philip to climb into the chariot and travel with him.

Before long, Philip and the man were deep in conversation about the words on the scroll as the chariot and its entourage rolled south. Philip explained how the words the man had been reading, about a sheep being led to slaughter and a man being mocked and put on trial, applied to Jesus, who had been crucified in the very city the man had just visited. With Philip's help, the Ethiopian soon acknowledged Jesus as the Messiah, the fulfillment of that scroll's prophecy. And when their journey took them alongside a stream (a minor miracle itself in that area), Philip baptized the man, acknowledging his faith in Jesus and his entry into the church.

The Ethiopian was on a journey. He hadn't arrived at his destination. He was still on the way when Philip met him, and that was okay. Philip joined the man on his journey, and traveled with him. Even after he was baptized, the Ethiopian had miles to go, but that, too, was okay.

The church is a place for people on a journey. Identification with a church doesn't mean you have arrived. Involvement in a church doesn't equate to reaching your destination. It is, however, a way to join others who are on similar—but not identical—journeys, and agree to travel together. Like the Ethiopian, you may have miles and miles to go, but that's okay, because church is a place for people who are on a journey, regardless of how far they've traveled or how far they have yet to go.

Church Is a Place to Receive (and Exercise) Acceptance and Patience

A fairly common attitude of people looking at churches from the outside is that they are filled with hypocritical, messed-up people who act like they have all the answers.

Other people, however, hold the opposite view. They think that churches are full of perfect people, people without problems, people who live buttoned-down, got-it-together lives that bear no resemblance to the gritty, chaotic, reality-based lives the rest of us live.

Whatever your impression of "church" may be, the chances are good that you're right. But the chances are even higher that there is more to the story than you might expect. Churches big and small alike are filled with all sorts of people. Whether a church hosts fifty worshipers every week or sees five thousand in attendance, you can reliably expect to find people fitting both descriptions—and everything in between.

After all, in the First Church of Jerusalem, described in the early chapters of Acts, there were all the following:

- Spiritually mature people, like Andrew, James, Philip, and Mary;[13]
- Physically-challenged people;[14]
- Former (and current) convicts, like Peter and John;[15]
- Religious professionals (priests and Levites);[16]
- Hypocrites, like Ananias and Sapphira;[17]
- Widows and foreigners;[18]
- Problems and problem-solvers;[19]
- Leaders, managers, and followers.[20]

And that was just one church, described in the first few chapters of Acts! These days, even the most homogeneous church is likely to include people of all sorts, making it an ideal place to receive—and exercise—acceptance and patience. For example:

Everyone in the church has sinned. The Bible teaches that every human being is in the same boat: "Everyone has sinned; we all fall short of God's glorious standard."[21] Some may act like that doesn't apply to them. Many may have found forgiveness and cleansing through their faith in Jesus. And a few may even lead such exemplary lives that they make Mother Teresa look like a train wreck. But none of that changes the fact that everyone in every church has sinned, though any and all can find forgiveness through faith in Jesus Christ—and any and all can and should extend the same kind of forgiveness to others.

Everyone in the church is a hypocrite. A common criticism of the church is that it is full of hypocrites. A *hypocrite* is a person who puts on a false appearance of virtue, or a person whose behavior contradicts what he or she claims to believe. According to that definition, all of us—in the church or outside the church—are hypocritical to one degree or another. That is, none of us lives in a way that is 100 percent consistent with what we believe or say we believe. For example, many people believe and teach our children that lying is wrong; yet we lie far more than we like to admit, excusing our dishonesty in all sorts of ways ("It was a white lie," we may say, or "everyone lies about *that*"). Or, to choose another example, some of us believe that God exists, and that He hears and answers prayer...but we seldom pray. If we were totally consistent with our beliefs, wouldn't we pray much more than we do? None of this is intended to excuse our hypocrisy, but simply to acknowledge that none of us lives completely consistent with our beliefs and ideals. One of the reasons struggling people attend church, however, is to enlist in the process of growing to be more like Jesus, who commands and teaches His followers not to be hypocritical.[22]

Everyone in the church is broken. From the very start, the church has been a gathering of sick and broken people. The earliest chapters of church history say, "[People] came from the villages surrounding Jerusalem, throngs of them, bringing the sick and bedeviled. And they all were healed."[23] Miraculous healings may not seem as common in most churches today, but the church continues to be a gathering of broken people. In almost any church, you will find people who are hurting and sick. You will see people who have endured divorce or depression. People who are dealing with difficult children and aging parents. People who are bedeviled by worry and fear. People who are trying to cope with dysfunctions and disorders. You will also find people who are being healed, who in their weakness and brokenness are finding God's strength and experiencing His power in their lives.

These realities open the church to a lot of criticism. Mahatma Gandhi, the "father" of an independent India, is often quoted as saying, "I like your Christ. I do not like your Christians. They are so unlike your Christ." His words still resonate today, more than a half-century after Gandhi's death. Every church in the world is likely to include people who are "unlike" Christ. That is an indictment, certainly; after all, Jesus said, "Students are to be like their teacher, and slaves are to be like their master."[24] True followers of Jesus should be growing every day more and more like their Teacher and Master.

But there is another side to that story. Since every church is filled with those who have sinned but are finding and extending forgiveness, hypocrites who have enlisted in the process of becoming more consistently like Jesus, and broken people who are experiencing God's healing power in various ways, every church is also a fine forum for receiving acceptance and patience.

You may approach church with some reservations. You may be all-too-aware of your own faults and failings. You may fear judgment and rejection. You may imagine that the church is filled with people who have it all together in ways that you do not. But you may be surprised. You may find acceptance where you expected judgment. You may find "church folk" to be far more patient with your sinfulness and brokenness than you ever could have guessed. If so, it shouldn't be all that surprising, because everyone you meet in the church is dealing with sin, hypocrisy, and brokenness, too.

And there is one more facet to the exploration process. The church not only offers a chance to experience acceptance and patience from others; it also offers ample opportunity to extend acceptance and patience to others. You may encounter Hazel, who sits in the same pew every Sunday, and snores through the pastor's sermons; you may have the chance to flash her a smile when she wakes in time for the last few minutes of the worship service. You may run into Bruce, who seems to have a knack for saying the wrong thing and rubbing people the wrong way, but whose day could be brightened by your willingness to listen. You may meet Seth, who breaks away from his exhausted single mom and dashes for the parking lot; you may be just in time to steer him back to safety.

It is strange how people can simultaneously see church as a place for perfect people and a gathering of awful people. In truth, of course, it is neither—or both. The church is a gathering of all kinds of people, a place to ask questions and seek answers, a place where everyone is on a journey of some kind, and a place that provides the opportunity to both experience and exercise acceptance and patience.

"MEN LABOR UNDER A MISTAKE…LAYING UP TREASURES WHICH MOTH AND RUST WILL CORRUPT AND THIEVES BREAK THROUGH AND STEAL. IT IS A FOOL'S LIFE."
—HENRY DAVID THOREAU

CHAPTER 2

FOCUS

It happens slowly. Gradually.

For a long time, you don't even notice anything different. But then one day it occurs to you, maybe while you're driving the car: You used to be able to read those signs at this distance. But now the words are blurry. The letters run into each other. It's all an indistinct blob.

You may chalk it up to sleepiness or allergies at first, but sooner or later you make an appointment with an optometrist. The doctor places in front of you something that looks like a medieval torture device. He instructs you to look through it.

You hear a click and you see the eye chart across the room. "Is that better?" the doctor says.

Another click, and the chart becomes clearer. "Or worse?"

"The first one was better," you say.

Then, another click. "Better?"

Click. "Or worse?"

You answer again.

The process is repeated several times, and then it begins anew with your other eye. You're not exactly sure what is being accomplished, but you feel like the two of you are getting somewhere.

And you are, it turns out. Before long (though you could have done without the eye drops and bright lights), the doctor confirms that you need glasses or contacts. You may be nearsighted or farsighted. Your vision may need help all the time or just for certain activities. But the first time you put on the proper prescription, it is amazing what happens. The world is clear again. Everything comes into focus. Blurry objects become distinct once more.

It is remarkable how different things look when you're wearing the right pair of glasses or contacts. The same sort of thing can happen in life, as well.

Maybe you've seen the television commercial that says, "Life comes at you fast." It is true. Most of us are speeding through our days, weeks, and lives at a breakneck speed. We have more choices than ever before: more work, more play, more distractions, more interruptions, more motion and commotion— more of everything. We are always busy, but never finished; always running, but never arriving; always active, but never getting anywhere.

Marty found a rare moment of reflection in a local coffee shop, where he explained to Calvin, a friend and coworker, "I have so much going on these days, I don't know whether I'm coming or going. It never stops, you know?" He sipped his drink. "I used to know what I wanted out of life. I used to have a sense of where I wanted to go. But I'm just so confused anymore. I really feel like I need to clear my head and figure out a whole bunch of stuff, you know? Get some perspective, maybe."

Marty may not know it, but his desire is extremely common these days. It is also a good answer to the question, "Why Church?"

Church Can Restore Your Rhythm

If you could travel back in time—say, to fifty or sixty years ago—you would notice some interesting differences between people's lifestyles in the 1950s or 1960s and our lifestyles these days. For example, a couple of generations ago, telephones were stationary things; they hung on walls or sat on desks and tables. News was available at certain times; in the morning newspaper, for example, or on the evening television newscast. Stores opened and closed each day, and most were closed all day Sunday.

How different from today. Telephones go everywhere we go, and make us accessible to people (and them to us) twenty-four hours a day, not to mention the dizzying array of additional tasks our phones may perform, from e-mail and information gathering to functioning as an alarm clock, map, or reading device. News comes to you instantly and constantly, via text messages, e-mail, websites, blogs, video, and more. And, of course, many stores, restaurants, and other businesses do a brisk business on Sundays.

Those are just a few of the changes in recent years, changes that have blurred the lines in our lives between work week and weekend, between waking and sleeping, on and off, and open and closed. Those are just some of the reasons people like Marty feel like they don't know whether they're coming or going. If there is no meaningful distinction between one day and another, between office and home, or between "connected" or "disconnected," then there is no difference between coming or going and no separation between here and there.

Many centuries ago, God told his people, "Six days you shall labor, and do all your work, but the seventh day is a Sabbath to the LORD your God."[1] God designed a pattern for us, a rhythm that would define, regulate, and inform our lives. He intended for human beings to enjoy regular periods of rest and worship—one out of every seven days. Six days of work, one day of rest and worship. He even went so far as to prescribe similar patterns of holidays and vacations (called "feasts" or "festivals" in the Bible) as well as a "year of Jubilee" to take place every fifty years (or roughly once every generation). Those guidelines served a religious purpose, of course, but they also provided a pace and tempo to people's lives that has largely disappeared in our day and age.

Golf pros will tell you that the backswing is as key to your golf game as your follow-through. Archers can tell you that the draw, the act of pulling back on the bowstring before release, is critical to a successful shot. Musicians know that music happens not only in the notes that are played or sung, but also in the silent rests between sounds.

The same is true in your week and in your life. Regular attendance and involvement in a church can return a necessary rhythm to your life. It can insert a meaningful sacred time and place into the otherwise hectic pace of your week. It can become for you a "reference point," a line to separate coming from going, so to speak; a chance to catch your breath at least once a week and gather strength for the week to come.

And that's just the beginning. It can do still more than that.

Church Can Adjust Your Focus

Henry David Thoreau famously wrote, "The mass of men lead lives of quiet desperation."[2] Those words are often quoted, of course, but less familiar to most people is the context in which he made that statement. He painted a picture that may have resonated with Marty, though couched in the farming culture of Thoreau's day:

> I see young men, my townsmen, whose misfortune it is to have inherited farms, houses, barns, cattle, and farming tools; for these are more easily acquired than got rid of. Better if they had been born in the open pasture and suckled by a wolf, that they might have seen with clearer eyes what field they were called to labor in. Who made them serfs of the soil? Why should they eat their sixty acres, when man is condemned to eat only his peck of dirt? Why should they begin digging their graves as soon as they are born? They have got to live a man's life, pushing all these things before them, and get on as well as they can. How many a poor immortal soul have I met well-nigh crushed and smothered under its load, creeping down the road of life, pushing before it a barn seventy-five feet by forty, its Augean stables never cleansed, and one hundred acres of land, tillage, mowing, pasture, and woodlot! The portionless, who struggle with no such unnecessary inherited encumbrances, find it labor enough to subdue and cultivate a few cubic feet of flesh.
>
> But men labor under a mistake. The better part of the man is soon plowed into the soil for compost. By a seeming fate, commonly called necessity, they are employed, as it says in an old book, laying up treasures which moth and rust will corrupt and thieves break through and steal. It is a fool's life.[3]

Thoreau looked across the landscape of nineteenth-century New England and saw a mass of men and women, like Marty, who labor day after day and week after week, getting on as well as they can, with little or no awareness of their purpose and potential. And he might be more amazed by our twenty-first century lifestyles; like the implements of farm life, an unexamined, workaday life is "more easily acquired than got rid of."

None of us intentionally embarks on "a fool's life," of course. It's just that life happens. And it happens so daily, unremittingly. We needed an education, so we went to school. We needed a job, so we applied and interviewed. We needed to pay the bills, so we worked hard. And we kept going. And going. Like Marty, we used to know what we wanted out of life; we used to have a sense of where we wanted to go. But somewhere along the line, we more or less lost our way. We lost focus.

The Bible contains a fascinating account of an incident in the life of the ancient prophet Elisha. There were many prophets in Israel during Elisha's lifetime, but he had been the faithful apprentice to Elijah, the great prophet who battled King Ahab and his queen, Jezebel. So, when Elijah ascended to heaven in a fiery chariot, Elisha took his mantle (literally) and became his successor.

When war erupted between Israel and Aram, Elisha became a valuable advisor to the king of Israel, alerting him to the movements and strategies of the Aramean armies. Elisha's prophetic insights enabled the armies of Israel to anticipate and counter everything the Arameans tried.

Soon it became obvious to the king of Aram that something fishy was going on. He called his senior officers together and demanded to know who among them was betraying their military secrets to the enemy.

"It is not coming from us," one of the officers said. "It is the prophet Elisha. Somehow he knows everything, and tells the king of Israel what you say even in the privacy of your bedroom!"

So the king of Aram issued an executive order for his troops to find Elisha and report his location. Before long, his location was pinpointed and a huge Aramean force was dispatched to surround the town where Elisha was staying.

When the next day dawned, Elisha's assistant stepped outside and saw Aramean chariots, horses, and soldiers on every side. He dashed back inside.

"We're surrounded!" he told the prophet. "The enemy is everywhere! What are we going to do?"

Elisha responded to his assistant's panic with a smile. "Don't be afraid," he said. "We still outnumber them."

The assistant may have questioned the prophet's sanity, but Elisha led him out of the house and extended his hands, palms upward. "Oh, Lord," he said, "Open his eyes. Let him see what I see!"

The younger man lifted his gaze. He focused on the hills behind and beyond the Aramean army, and saw a vast array of horses and chariots of fire surrounding the enemy. The prophet was right; the Arameans were outnumbered...and surrounded. Then Elisha prayed for the Aramean armies to be blinded, and they were. The entire force was captured and presented to the king of Israel, and the war between Israel and Aram ended.[4] The prophet's prayer didn't change reality. His words didn't make the horses and chariots of fire appear; they had always been there on the hillside surrounding the Aramean army. But Elisha's prayer adjusted and enlarged his assistant's vision.

That's what regular church attendance and involvement can do for you. It can adjust and enlarge your vision. Regular participation in Christian worship and teaching can change your focus, supply a new awareness of your purpose and potential, and offer cohesive answers to the most fundamental questions of life:

- *Who am I?* Am I a "serf of the soil," as Thoreau put it? Am I a cog in a machine? Is my identity merely a reflection of what I do? Am I defined by my family of origin? by my job? by my roles as son or daughter, single or married, husband or wife, mother or father? Or is there a better way to answer that question? Does it have something to do with being created in God's image? Does my sense of identity reflect how others see me, how I see myself, or how God sees me?
- *What's wrong with me?* Why do I do the things I do? Why am I so often angry? or sad? Why do I end up hurting those I love most? Is there something wrong inside me? Is it just

me, or is everyone like this? Why do some people seem to have it all together, while I feel like I'm limping along in many ways?

- *How do I fix what's wrong with me?* Is it possible to "fix" the things that hold me back and hold me down? Is there a better life for me? Is there a way to find forgiveness and freedom, healing and wholeness?

- *Why am I here?* There's got to be something more than working and paying the bills and getting older, right? Am I laying up treasures, where "moth and rust destroy, and where thieves break in and steal?"(See Matthew 6:19, NASB). Am I living a fool's life? Or is there a reason for my existence? Is there a purpose I haven't yet discovered?

- *Where am I going?* Am I destined only to be "plowed into the soil for compost," as Thoreau said? Or is there something more than this life—something beyond this? And even if there is, is it really possible to know?

Those questions cannot be answered all at once, of course. Nor are the answers likely to come in order. And the process of truly grasping and owning the answers to those questions will certainly look different for you than for others. But regular participation in Christian worship and teaching can go a long way toward the formation of a cohesive worldview, opening your eyes (as the prophet Elisha did for his assistant) to the things that are true and real in your life and world.

Church Can Lift Your Perspective

The comic strip Calvin and Hobbes featured the antics of a spike-haired boy, Calvin, and his stuffed tiger, Hobbes (who lived and spoke in Calvin's imagination). One pair of panels shows Calvin and Hobbes under a starlit night sky. Calvin says, "If people sat outside and looked at the stars each night, I'll bet they'd live a lot differently."

"How so?" says Hobbes.

Calvin answers, "Well, when you look into infinity, you realize that there are more important things than what people do all day."

He's right. Elisha's prayer did more than adjust his assistant's focus; it also lifted his perspective. In order to see the armies of the Lord, the horses and chariots of fire, the young man had to lift his gaze to the hills. Only then could he see the true nature of things. Only then was he enlightened.

The "poor immortal souls" of Thoreau's acquaintance never looked up from their hundred acres of "land, tillage, mowing, pasture, and woodlot" to the array of possibilities and freedoms he observed and enjoyed. Their perspective was downcast, so their potential was restricted.

Josh is a long-haul truck driver. Week after week, year after year, his life consisted of long hours, lengthy trips, and lingering doubts about the path he had chosen in life. In thirty-five years of life, he had entered a church only for weddings and funerals, until his wife badgered him into attending an Easter Sunday worship service with her and the children. He went begrudgingly, but was surprised to find that he enjoyed the experience. He was even more surprised when his wife introduced him to two other truckers. Soon they were swapping stories, laughs, and contact information. Over the next few months, he and his new friends stayed in touch, and he even learned of a larger network of Christian truckers who are answering some of his questions and helping him work through some of the challenges of his long-haul lifestyle. He still works long hours, but feels less alone on the road, far more connected to home, and much happier about his life and his future.

After her husband died, Edna seldom left her home...except to go to the doctor. Her ailments multiplied, as did her medications. She became more and more focused on her many aches and pains, and began to worry that she might die in her sleep some night. Before long, her life consisted of sleepless nights and fear-filled days. The first time a neighbor persuaded her to go to church, she slept through most of the service. But she returned the next week, and the week after that. Then one week her neighbor explained that she wouldn't be able to sit with Edna in the worship service because she volunteered in the nursery rocking babies once a month. Rather than sit alone in church, Edna accompanied her friend, and was soon a fixture in the nursery. She fell in love with the children, and they fell in love with her. Though she still has aches and pains, and takes daily medication for arthritis, she has discontinued her other prescriptions, and no longer has trouble sleeping at night.

Interestingly, neither Josh nor Edna was looking for spiritual answers when they first came to the church. Neither was particularly aware of any needs their souls might have had. In fact, while Edna became a follower of Jesus soon after she started attending church, Josh says he is still "thinking things through and feeling my way," spiritually speaking. But both experienced a shift in perspective when they began attending church.

Church lifted Edna's perspective from her depressing world of aches and pains, pills and prescriptions, and opened a door to new joy and purpose in caring for others. Josh's perspective also changed, as he discovered resources and connections he never knew were available. Participation in a healthy church can do something similar for you, even if you're not an over-the-road trucker or a semi-invalid.

Radio personality Ron Hutchcraft told this story on one of his radio programs:

> I talked not too long ago to a man whose wife had left him quite a while ago. She refuses to divorce him. She refuses to reconcile. And he's thought about that, day and night, for four years. Well, I listened, and then I gave him some unexpected advice. I said, "Mark, you need to get a place where you can serve the Lord and help some people. This has so occupied you, and understandably so, that you haven't had time to serve. Find some boys you can work with at church, or something you can do with the teenagers at church, or a Bible study you can lead, or volunteer for something. Because as you serve, you'll be able to see this situation better, and you'll know what God wants."
>
> Mark said, "You know, you're right. I've not served the Lord for a while because I've been so involved in this. I need to get busy for others."[5]

That was good advice. Especially during times of uncertainty and pain, we can quite easily become focused on ourselves, our hurts, and our needs. Involvement in church can lift your perspective and open new vistas to you. It can redirect your attention from yourself and your needs to others and their needs. It can teach you and give you practice in seeing things from a different perspective, a higher perspective.

Rhythm. Focus. Perspective. To paraphrase Thoreau, the mass of men and women today lead lives that are sorely lacking in those areas. They have so much going on, they don't know whether they're coming or going. They used to know what they wanted out of life, and where they wanted to go, but somewhere along the line, they lost their focus. They need a new perspective, a longer view. It is a need poetically expressed in the hymn by Sunday school teacher Priscilla Owens:

> Will your anchor hold in the storms of life,
> When the clouds unfold their wings of strife?
> When the strong tides lift, and the cables strain,
> Will your anchor drift or firm remain?

> We have an anchor that keeps the soul
> Steadfast and sure while the billows roll,
> Fastened to the Rock which cannot move,
> Grounded firm and deep in the Savior's love.

> It is safely moored, 'twill the storm withstand,
> For 'tis well secured by the Savior's hand;
> And the cables passed from His heart to mine,
> Can defy the blast, through strength divine.

> It will firmly hold in the straits of fear,
> When the breakers have told the reef is near;
> Though the tempest rave and the wild winds blow,
> Not an angry wave shall our bark o'erflow.

It will surely hold in the floods of death,
When the waters cold chill our latest breath;
On the rising tide it can never fail,
While our hopes abide within the veil.[6]

"THERE IS NO SATISFACTION THAT CAN COMPARE WITH LOOKING BACK ACROSS THE YEARS AND FINDING YOU'VE GROWN IN SELF-CONTROL, JUDGMENT, GENEROSITY, AND UNSELFISHNESS."

—ELLA WHEELER WILCOX

CHAPTER 3

DISCOVER

It was called the Corps of Discovery.

In 1803, American President Thomas Jefferson commissioned his private secretary, Meriwether Lewis, to form and lead a team of explorers through the vast Louisiana Territory, newly purchased from France. "The object of your mission," Jefferson wrote Lewis, "is to explore the Missouri River, and such principal streams of it, as, by its course and communication with the waters of the Pacific Ocean, whether the Columbia, Oregon, Colorado or any other river, may offer the most direct and practicable water communication across this continent, for the purposes of commerce."

Lewis recruited his friend, William Clark, and together with a forty-man team, they set off from St. Louis, Missouri, on May 14, 1804. It took them a year-and-a-half to reach the Pacific Coast, and they were forced to spend the winter at the mouth of the Columbia River near present-day Astoria, Oregon, before beginning their return trip in late March, 1806. The party finally arrived back in St. Louis on September 23, 1806, where they were lauded as heroes. Though they had been gone so long that many had given them up for dead, only one member of the team died (probably of a ruptured appendix) on the arduous journey.

The Corps of Discovery never found the desired "Northwest Passage" linking the Mississippi River to the Pacific Ocean. But they lived up to the name, nonetheless. They mapped immense areas of the northwest United States, naming rivers, creeks, and landmarks along the way. They catalogued forty-eight tribes of Native Americans. They documented 122 species of animals, birds, and fish that were previously unknown to science, from the Western pileated woodpecker to the coyote and the grizzly bear. They discovered 179 species of previously undocumented plants and trees. They returned with descriptions and drawings of the Great Plains and the Rocky Mountains, of teepees and Mandan lodges, of Great Falls and Pompey's Tower (renamed Pompey's pillar in 1814, a sandstone butte William Clark named after the son of Sacagawea, the Shoshone woman who guided and translated for a large portion of the journey), and more.

When the Corps of Discovery set out on their journey, they had high hopes, but little understanding of the adventures and delights, discoveries and breakthroughs that would characterize their journey. None could have known how it would change their lives—or how it would change the lives of others who would come after them.

So it is for you, as you seek answers to the question, "Why Church?" Participation and involvement in the life of a healthy church is a journey of discovery. It can yield unexpected adventures and delights, unforeseen fruits, and open the door to breakthroughs that can change your life—and the lives of others who might come after you.

Church Can Help You Discover God

"I can find God anywhere," Jamie told his friend Ben. He shared a cubicle at work with Ben, and the two had shared many conversations about God and church. Ben was a committed follower of Jesus; Jamie had always been skeptical of his friend's faith. "I can find Him in nature. In the stars and planets. I think I feel closest to God when I'm on horseback. I don't need a church to find God," Jamie said.

Ben nodded. "I agree."

"You do?"

He smiled. "I do. In fact, the Bible says something similar."

"It does?"

"Absolutely. It says that God's attributes are displayed in nature. Ever since the beginning of Creation, His beauty and power have been plain to anyone who cared to look."[1]

"All right, then." Jamie seemed pleased.

"It's called natural revelation, but it has its limits."

"Limits?"

As their conversation continued, Ben explained that a person can discover all sorts of things about God through nature. It reveals His beauty and His imagination, for example. But there is much more to be discovered than we can possibly learn through nature. Otherwise, God would not have sent His Son, Jesus, to be born and live, and then to die and rise again.

After His resurrection, Jesus met His closest followers on a mountain. He told them, "Go out and train everyone you meet, far and near, in this way of life, marking them by baptism in the threefold name: Father, Son, and Holy Spirit. Then instruct them in the practice of all I have commanded you. I'll be with you as you do this, day after day after day, right up to the end of the age."[2]

Soon after that, in the event that gave birth to the church, Jesus sent His Holy Spirit to energize and equip His followers for that task. In the days, weeks, months, and years ahead, the church began to do what Jesus had said, helping people of all kinds discover God and His ways.

On one occasion, two followers of Jesus named Paul and Silas were spreading the news and talking about Jesus in a prosperous Roman town called Philippi. They were arrested for disturbing the peace, beaten, and chained in a local prison overnight. Undaunted, Paul and Silas prayed and sang out loud, and were even joined by the other prisoners.

Sometime after midnight, the ground started to shudder. An earthquake shook the prison to its foundation. The chains broke free from the walls, and the cell doors clanged open.

In the strange silence that followed the tremors, the jailer appeared at the entrance to the prison and saw the heavy outer door lying atop rubble. He peered into the dark confines. He saw no one. He heard nothing.

Supposing that his prisoners had all escaped, and knowing the penalty for his empty jail would be death, he drew his sword. He turned its point on himself.

"Stop!" Paul's voice pierced the darkness. "Don't hurt yourself. We are all still here."

The jailer dropped his sword and found a nearby torch. He ducked into the prison and examined the cells. No one had escaped. He dropped to his knees before Paul and Silas, shaking with relief—and awe. He led them out into the moonlit night and turned to face them. "Please tell me: how can I be saved? Tell me what to do."

They answered, "Give yourself to Jesus. Trust Him. Follow Him. He will save you and everyone in your house!" (See Acts 16:12-34).

That Philippian jailer discovered the path to God that day. The path to deliverance, to salvation, to new life, and to the kind of power that can open prison doors and set prisoners free.

The jailer didn't have to go to church to discover those things. He found God through the church, nonetheless, because the church came to him—in the persons of Paul and Silas.

So it is today. Some people discover God and experience salvation through Jesus Christ during a church service. They may have walked down the aisle after a sermon, knelt at an altar, and experienced forgiveness, healing, and salvation while an organ or worship team played.

Others, however, discover God while watching a television show. Some do so at their kitchen table or at a concert or festival—even on a street corner or in a jail cell. However, in all but the rarest of instances, the church still played a part. They may have come to church...or the church may have come to them.

In fact, that very thing may be happening for you right now. However you received this book, God has used the church to get this book written, published, and into your hands. And He may even now—this moment—be speaking to you through His Holy Spirit's voice. He may be whispering in your ear. He may be drawing your heart closer and closer to His. If that happens to be the case, then you may be at a place where you want to consciously, intentionally, begin a new, living relationship with God through Jesus Christ. One way to take that step is to pray a simple prayer to God, in words like this:

> *God, I sense Your presence. I hear Your voice. I know You are here, and that You are speaking to me right now.*
>
> *You know me. You know me better than I know myself. You know that I'm a sinner. You know I need Your forgiveness.*

I know that, too, and I know that Jesus died to make forgiveness and new life possible for me. On the basis of what Jesus did on the cross, I ask You to forgive me and cleanse me of my sins.

Whatever questions I may still have, whatever doubts, I want to begin right now to know You and follow Jesus from this day forth. Come into my life and give me Your Holy Spirit to live in me and help me. In Jesus' name, amen.

If you prayed that prayer, the Bible says that you are a "new creation."[3] You have a brand new start. You have access to God by a "new and living way"[4] that Jesus provides for you. And, in many ways, your journey of discovery has only begun.

Church Can Help You Discover Yourself

His name is lost to us, but his first encounter with the church has been preserved.

He had never walked. Never run. Never jumped or skipped or danced. He had been crippled since birth, and had long been a familiar sight outside the Beautiful Gate, the entrance to the magnificent courts of the Jerusalem temple, where he sat, begging. His poverty and misfortune contrasted sharply with the dazzling brass and rich colors of the archway.

On this particular day, he watched the approach of two healthy Jewish men who had dropped money into his hands in the past. He called out loudly and begged them for *alms,* a donation that would not only help him, but would also constitute a *mitzvah*—an act of righteousness—for them.

They stopped. He lifted his dirty palm in the air, but humbly fastened his gaze on the pavement in front of him.

One of the men spoke. "Look at us."

He looked up.

"We have no money. But we will give you what we have. In the name of Jesus Christ of Nazareth, stand up! Walk!" Then he reached out his hand, inviting the beggar to grasp it in order to stand.

The beggar hesitated. He searched the man's face for a sign of mockery or anger, but there was none.

Several worshipers paused and watched as he gripped the strong man's hand. The man gripped his elbow with his other hand and pulled him up, and as he did so, the beggar felt something in his legs—something he couldn't remember ever having felt before. It was strength.

His legs unfolded beneath him, and his twisted ankles straightened. He looked down. His bare feet stood flat on the ground. His legs were holding him up.

The man released his grip, and for the first time in the beggar's life, he took a step! Then another. He looked at the two men, who were smiling broadly. They slapped his back and laughed.

He extended himself to his full height and leaped into the air as though he expected to take flight. Then he laughed, too, and when the men turned to go, he entered the temple courts with them, walking and laughing and leaping and praising God for his healing.

That beggar's first encounter with Jesus Christ's healing power came through the church. The two men he met that day outside the temple's Beautiful Gate were Peter and John, who had recently (perhaps just the day before) experienced the intoxicating birth of the church on the day of Pentecost. The healing of the beggar is the first recorded miracle of the brand new church.[5]

It is also informative because it illustrates what many people experience when they encounter the church. They may be crippled, hindered, and held back in some way. They may want nothing more than a little practical help. They may know little or nothing of Jesus. Like that beggar, they may have taken no visible steps of faith, but they are willing to reach out, hear more, and maybe believe just a little bit. And in that act, they often not only discover something of God, but something of themselves as well.

One of the reasons the church exists is to help faulty men and women experience Jesus in all His perfection and purity...and to help them "grow in the grace and knowledge of our Lord and Savior Jesus Christ."[6] Many refer to this process as "spiritual growth."

It is a learning process. A growing process. A journey of becoming more and more of what God designed you to be.

C. S. Lewis once wrote,

> The more we...let [God] take over, the more truly ourselves we become... Our real selves are all waiting for us in Him. It is no good trying to 'be myself' without Him. The more I resist Him and try to live on my own, the more I become dominated by my own heredity and upbringing and surroundings and natural desires. In fact what I so proudly call 'Myself' becomes merely the meeting place for trains of events which I never started and which I cannot stop. What I call 'My wishes' become merely the desires thrown up by my physical organism or pumped into me by other men's thoughts or even suggested to me by the devils... I am not, in my natural state, nearly so much of a person as I like to believe: most of what I call 'me' can be very easily explained. It is when I turn to Christ, when I give myself up to His personality, that I first begin to have a real personality of my own.[7]

This process of discovering and becoming who God created you and intended for you to be is likely to be as unique as you are. No one on earth is exactly like you, and your journey of discovery will involve finding the practices and habits that help you grow in the grace and knowledge of our Lord and Savior Jesus Christ. These may include the following:

- private and public worship
- Bible studies and accountability groups
- private prayer practices and corporate prayer gatherings
- acts of service to God and others
- giving your money, time, and talents to God's work
- spiritual disciplines, such as fasting and meditation
- sacraments (e.g., baptism and communion), rituals, and reminders
- ministry and leadership

Some of the above will be touched on later in this book.

However, all are available in and through the life and work of the church and provide the means and method for your spiritual growth and development.

Church Can Help You Discover God's Word

When Ben and Jamie talked about finding God in nature, they were discussing one of the ways God has revealed Himself to humanity. Theologians call it natural revelation. There is another way, however, that is both more specific and more comprehensive. It is called special revelation, and it refers to the ways God has revealed Himself to us in writings, which have been preserved through millennia as Scripture—the Bible.

When Philip met the Ethiopian on the Gaza road, as mentioned earlier, the man in the chariot was reading from the writings of Isaiah, one of the ancient Hebrew prophets. The Ethiopian was an intelligent man. He was extremely well educated and influential in the highest government circles. He had made a pilgrimage to worship at the temple in Jerusalem. Yet he welcomed help from Philip, a former fisherman from Galilee, to understand the Scripture and apply it to his life.

Just as Philip served that Ethiopian official, the church today can serve you by helping you discover, study, and apply God's Word. It can happen as you listen to and take notes on the weekend Bible messages that are offered in worship services. It can take place as you participate in Bible studies and seminars the church may offer. It can even occur in the midst of conversation as you're serving with others who share what they've been studying and learning from the Bible. As Paul once told his younger coworker Timothy,

> There's nothing like the written Word of God for showing you the way to salvation through faith in Christ Jesus. Every part of Scripture is God-breathed and useful one way or another—showing us truth, exposing our rebellion, correcting our mistakes, training us to live God's way. Through the Word we are put together and shaped up for the tasks God has for us.[8]

In just sixty-four words (in the above paraphrase), Paul mentions six treasures to be discovered in the Bible.

The Bible can show you the way to salvation. Wherever you are in your spiritual journey, careful and sincere study of the Bible will reveal to you that new life in Christ is available to you "by grace...through faith,"[9] assure you that "everyone who calls on the name of the Lord will be saved,"[10] and exhort you to "put your entire trust in the Master Jesus [and learn to] live as you were meant to live."[11]

The Bible can show you truth. The sixty-six books of the Bible contain poetry and proverbs, songs and hymns, history and philosophy, parables and prophecy, letters and dreams and visions...but it is all truth. It doesn't merely contain truth; it is truth. It takes study and skill to understand and interpret it, but as Paul told Timothy, it is "God-breathed," truth upon truth from beginning to end.

The Bible can expose your rebellion. When the first humans rebelled against God in the Garden of Eden, the Bible says they "heard the sound of the LORD God as he was walking in the garden in the cool of the day, and they hid from the LORD God among the trees of the garden."[12] But God called out to them, and asked a series of questions that helped them confront their sin. His written Word today does what His spoken words did in the Garden: It helps us confront the ways we have rebelled and sinned against God—not to make us feel guilty, but to lead us into forgiveness and freedom.

The Bible can correct your mistakes. Once when a group of Jesus' critics were trying to trip Him up with a theological question, He answered, "You are mistaken, because you do not know the Scriptures."[13] Bible study and Bible knowledge won't prevent every mistake, but together with sincere submission to God, it can correct many of your mistakes and help you to make fewer in the future.

The Bible can train you to live God's way. A baseball outfielder shags one fly ball after another. A boxer pummels a punching bag. A musician practices scales over and over again. They do these things to train themselves to catch, fight, or play well when the time comes. Similarly, reading and studying the Bible trains the human heart, soul, and mind in "being holy and good before God as long as we live."[14]

The Bible can assemble and shape you for the tasks God has for you. Believe it or not, you possess talents and skills that God wants to use in the church and in the world. Not only that, but if you have experienced new life through faith in Jesus Christ, you have been given a spiritual gift that God wants you to discover, develop, and use to serve Him. Reading and studying the Bible is one way to do that, which leads to the final point of this chapter.

Church Can Help You Discover Your Spiritual Gifts

If you are a follower of Jesus Christ, you not only have natural skills (such as carpentry) and talents (such as an eye for design); you also have a spiritual gift. According to the Bible, you received a spiritual gift—and maybe several—when the Holy Spirit took up residence in your heart and life. And discovering and using your spiritual gift (or gifts) will introduce you to a level of fun and fulfillment and growth in your spiritual life that you never knew were possible.

But how do you discover your spiritual gift? There are several answers to that question, and most involve the help and participation of a church family:

Prayer. First, you can ask God to help you discover your spiritual gift(s). He knows you better than anyone, and He knows your gifts as well since He gave them to you.

Bible study. "Through the Word we are put together and shaped up for the tasks God has for us."[15] In fact, the Bible contains several listings of spiritual gifts (see: Romans 12:6–8 and 1 Corinthians 12:1–11).

Trial and error. Your church offers many opportunities to try various areas and roles of service. Some people have many areas of interest, and must try several in order to narrow things down and learn to distinguish between "interest" and "giftedness."

Observation and counsel. Your church also offers a fine resource for discernment in the form of mature Christians who know you, have observed you, and who can offer suggestions as to what your spiritual gift(s) might be.

Assessment tools. A number of spiritual gift assessments are available in books and workbooks, as well as online. Your pastor or Bible study leader can probably guide you to an assessment tool he or she has used in the past. However, keep in mind that while most assessments will help you discover your spiritual gifts, which are outlined in the Bible, God may also have gifted you with talents such as musicianship, songwriting, painting/sculpture, hospitality, or website design. So, don't overlook such skills and talents either.

If you intend to follow Jesus and discover all that God wants you to learn, know, do, and enjoy, you can do no better than to join God's "Corps of Discovery": the church. It is a team effort, like that of Lewis and Clark, but one that will help you discover and develop in ways you could not do alone.

"SOMETIMES YOU WANT TO GO WHERE EVERYBODY KNOWS YOUR NAME."

—GARY PORTNOY AND JUDY HART ANGELO

CHAPTER 4

BELONG

Everyone needs something.

Some of us don't like to admit it. We recoil from the notion. We like to think of ourselves as independent and self-sufficient. We imagine ourselves as the subject of William Ernest Henley's poem "Invictus":

> Out of the night that covers me,
> Black as the Pit from pole to pole,
> I thank whatever gods may be
> For my unconquerable soul.
>
> In the fell clutch of circumstance
> I have not winced nor cried aloud.
> Under the bludgeonings of chance
> My head is bloody, but unbowed.
>
> Beyond this place of wrath and tears
> Looms but the Horror of the shade,
> And yet the menace of the years
> Finds, and shall find, me unafraid.
>
> It matters not how strait the gate,
> How charged with punishments the scroll.
> I am the master of my fate:
> I am the captain of my soul.[1]

It makes good poetry, but it is poor theology and lousy psychology. Like it or not, you have needs. A couple of generations ago, American psychologist Abraham Maslow formulated a hierarchy of basic human needs. He suggested that all human beings strive constantly to fulfill certain needs, and we will do so in a particular, predictable order. Our most basic needs, of course, are physical: food, water, sleep, breath, etc. When those needs are met, Maslow said humans instinctively and unavoidably seek safety and security—in our persons, as well as in employment, health, property, and so on.

Next on his hierarchy (usually depicted as a pyramid) is the need to be loved and to belong, and the need to associate with others and fit in. To one degree or another, every human being longs to belong—somewhere. We want to feel a part of something and to feel important to someone.

This need is evident in the very first pages of the Bible. When God created the first man, he allowed that man to become aware of his uniqueness and aloneness, and then sedated him and created the first woman. When the man awoke and met the woman, do you know what he said? His first words weren't "Yeah, baby!" or "How do you do?" His first words, recorded in Genesis 2, were, "Bone from my bone, and flesh from my flesh!"[2] In other words, "We have so much in common! We belong to each other! We fit together!"

And just as God kindly and lovingly created the first humans to fill each other's need for belonging (among other things), he has also provided the church to meet that need.

Church Can Be a "Third Place"

When the television sitcom *Cheers* debuted in 1982, it underscored for many people a momentous change that had occurred in the preceding generations. *Cheers* depicted a Boston bar where a cast of regulars gathered to drink, eat, relax, chat, joke, fight, and make up. It was a place "where everybody knows your name," as its famous theme song said; the kind of place many in the television audience lacked. Some have called it a "third place"—somewhere to belong besides work and home.

The end of World War II saw the rise of a new way of life in the United States—and in other parts of the Western world. Soldiers and sailors returned from war, families were reunited, and many moved out of urban areas into sprawling "suburbs," with yards and garages and cul-de-sacs. Ray Oldenburg, in his influential book, *The Great Good Place,* pointed out:

> Life in the subdivision may have satisfied the combat veteran's longing for a safe, orderly, and quiet haven, but it rarely offered the sense of place and belonging that had rooted his parents and grandparents. Houses alone do not a community make, and the typical subdivision proved hostile to the emergence of any structure or space utilization beyond the uniform houses and streets that characterized it.
>
> Like all-residential city blocks, observed one student of the American condition, the suburb is "merely a base from which the individual reaches out to the scattered components of social existence." Though proclaimed as offering the best of both rural and urban life, the automobile suburb had the effect of fragmenting the individual's world. As one observer wrote, "A man works in one place, sleeps in another, shops somewhere else, finds pleasure or companionship where he can, and cares about none of these places.[3]

As another diagnostician, Richard Goodwin, says, we now live in a day and age where "there is virtually no place where neighbors can anticipate unplanned meetings—no pub, or corner store, or park."[4] That is a societal shortcoming the church is ideally equipped to fill.

Whether you are a single person who longs for someplace besides bars to meet other singles your age, or an overworked businessperson who really needs to "get a life," or a frazzled parent who hungers for adult conversation, the church can be a "third place" for you. It can be a way to bring together "the scattered components of social existence" for you—a place to find acceptance, friendship, and community with people of similar interests and values.

Church Can Be Like a Store

A large church in Cincinnati, Ohio, hosts thousands of enthusiastic worshipers in a building that once housed an HQ home improvement store. It might be fun to know if there were any people who entered the renovated building in its early months expecting to shop at a commercial outlet.

But many newcomers and visitors to churches enter that way, anyway. It is natural when checking out a church for the first time to approach it as a consumer, like a "shopper" who is looking for a good value. *Are the kids' programs any good? Will I like the music? Will the preacher put me to sleep? Where are the bathrooms? Does this church have a women's group? A youth ministry? A motorcycle club?*

In that respect and others, a church can be like a store. For example, first impressions are important. Another similarity is that most people like to feel welcome, but don't want to be singled out or embarrassed. And, of course, location makes a difference, too.

As important as such concerns may be, however, they are not great reasons for choosing a church. There is a fundamental difference between a store and a church: a store wants to keep you coming back as a customer, while the purpose of the church is to make you an owner—of the message and the mission. What Jesus told His first followers applies to everyone who discovers new life through faith in Him: "Go out and train everyone you meet, far and near, in this way of life, marking them by baptism in the threefold name: Father, Son, and Holy Spirit. Then instruct them in the practice of all I have commanded you."[5]

Church Can Be Like a Hospital

As discussed in chapter one, you will meet all kinds of people in church. Men, women, children, strong, weak, short, tall, round, "square," uptight, and more. Some of the people you meet will be sweet; some may not. Some will be obviously struggling with addictions and dysfunctions; others may be struggling just as much, but not visibly. Some will be "rough around the edges," and others will seem to have nothing but edges. And some will be just like you, like it or not.

But of one thing you can be sure: everyone in the church has been stricken with the same disease—sin. For as the Bible says,

> Everyone has sinned; we all fall short of God's glorious standard. Yet God...through Christ Jesus...freed us from the penalty for our sins. For God presented Jesus as the sacrifice for sin. People are made right with God when they believe that Jesus sacrificed his life, shedding his blood. This sacrifice shows that God was being fair when he held back and did not punish those who sinned in times past, for he was looking ahead and including them in what he would do in this present time.[6]

As M. Craig Barnes has said, "The Reformers claimed that the church would always be a hospital for sinners. This means that we cannot expect its members to be spiritually healthy."[7] This is why no church is perfect. It is also why no church should aspire to be perfect because that would mean it had ceased to be a hospital for sinners.

So, if you don't have it all together, the church is for you. If you feel wounded, sick, and sore, the church is for you. If you struggle with doubts, the church is for you. If you have a temper, the church is for you. If you're a mess, the church is for you. If you're worse than most or better than most, the church is for you. It is a hospital for sinners, an infirmary for the hurting, and a hospice for the dying (and we are all terminal).

However, the church is also different from a hospital, in that the "doctors" and "nurses" are also patients...and the patients are all called to play a role in the healing and recovery of others. As the Bible says,

> The God of all comfort...comforts us in all our troubles, so that we can comfort those in any trouble with the comfort we ourselves receive from God. For just as we

share abundantly in the sufferings of Christ, so also our comfort abounds through Christ. If we are distressed, it is for your comfort and salvation; if we are comforted, it is for your comfort, which produces in you patient endurance of the same sufferings we suffer. And our hope for you is firm, because we know that just as you share in our sufferings, so also you share in our comfort.[8]

Church Can Be Like a Club

Several generations ago, various clubs and fraternal organizations thrived throughout many countries: Boy Scouts and Girl Scouts, Kiwanis, Rotary, Optimists, Lions, Masons, Elks, Moose, Odd Fellows, Knights of Columbus, Shriners, Daughters of the American Revolution, Sons of the American Revolution, Chautauqua Institution, not to mention college fraternities, sororities, and similar organizations. Such groups provided the opportunity to unite for a common cause and simultaneously enjoy the company of like-minded people.

These days, of course, many associations like those above have shrunk or disappeared entirely. But that's not because people no longer want to pursue a common purpose and find camaraderie with others of similar interests; it is more likely due to the hectic pace of modern life and perhaps also the rise of suburban and exurban lifestyles.

However, the church survives and still offers the opportunity for people to experience common cause and purposeful pursuits. In that respect, of course, a church can be much like a club, lodge, or service organization. It is, however, substantially different.

Clubs and other organizations exist primarily for the benefit of their members. The members pay dues and fees and, in return, receive the benefit and services of the club. Not so with the church. The church exists not for the benefit of its members, but for the benefit of others. It exists for the sake of those *outside* "the club." The church is the embodiment of Jesus Christ on earth and its mission is to fulfill *His* mission, which He revealed at the very beginning of His earthly ministry when He read from

the prophecy of Isaiah in His hometown synagogue, saying,
"The Spirit of the Lord is upon me,
for he has anointed me to bring Good News to the poor.
He has sent me to proclaim that captives will be released,
that the blind will see,
that the oppressed will be set free,
and that the time of the Lord's favor has come."[9]

So, while the church is a great place to unite with others around a common purpose, that purpose is not solely for the benefit of those in the church, but also for those who are still waiting to receive the Good News, to experience release, to be given their sight, and to be set free.

Church Can Be Like a School

Schools are places of learning. So are churches.

Your church may host Sunday school every week, for all ages, from the cradle to the grave. Chances are, a sizeable portion of your church's worship gatherings is devoted to hearing and learning what God says to us in the Bible. Your church may offer weeknight Bible studies, small-group gatherings, weekend seminars, and more. Your church may meet in a school, or may even *be* a school, providing a wholesome education for kids of all ages. Some churches even offer college and seminary courses.

Most churches today offer a dazzling array of educational opportunities:

- Financial Peace and money management seminars
- Preparing-for-Marriage studies for engaged couples
- The Art of Marriage, Fireproof Your Marriage, and other marriage-strengthening studies
- GodQuest and other resources for defending the faith
- leadership studies and resources
- recovery groups and resources (for dealing with grief, addiction, etc.)
- cultural studies and worldview development resources
- Becoming a Contagious Christian and other how-to-share-your-faith studies, and more.

If you hang around most churches for any length of time, you'll probably be able to participate in a helpful study on almost any topic that interests you.

But the church is—and always should be—much more than a place to learn. Unlike a school, the church's "product" is not education; it is *transformation*. The purpose of every Bible study, small-group meeting, and Sunday school class in the church is ultimately to show the way to salvation through faith in Christ Jesus and to train us to live God's way. (See *The Message*, 2 Timothy 3:15–16, for more information.)

Church can be that for you. It can be a place of learning and much more. It can be a transforming experience—life-giving, life-changing.

Church Can Be Like a Family

One of the most common figures of speech people use to refer to the church is that of a family. Many call it a "family of faith"—and it is.

"God sets the lonely in families," the Bible says,[10] and the church has been His intended means for doing that for two millennia. The Bible refers to the church as "the household of faith"[11] and "family of believers."[12] Writing to non-Jewish followers of Jesus in Ephesus, Paul said, "You Gentiles are no longer strangers and foreigners. You are citizens along with all of God's holy people. You are members of God's family."[13]

However, there is a key difference between the church and the family—a *huge* difference. Families are closed circles. The membership is limited. You're either in or out. And, while it is possible to expand the family by marriage or birth, it is typically a long (and even painful) process.

Not so with the church. The gospel of Matthew, the first of the four Bible books that tell the life story of Jesus, relates an exchange Jesus had during His teaching ministry:

> As Jesus was speaking to the crowd, his mother and brothers stood outside, asking to speak to him. Someone told Jesus, "Your mother and your brothers

are outside, and they want to speak to you."

Jesus asked, "Who is my mother? Who are my brothers?" Then he pointed to his disciples and said, "Look, these are my mother and brothers. Anyone who does the will of my Father in heaven is my brother and sister and mother!"[14]

To our ears, of course, it sounds like Jesus was being rude to his mother and brothers, refusing to see them. It sounds like he was upset at being interrupted. Or maybe he reacted against an apparent plea for special privileges. Perhaps he discerned a little power play in their insistence that he take orders from them.

But that wasn't really the case at all. There is no reason to believe that Jesus was annoyed in any way. He was simply using the interruption as a teaching opportunity, a chance to get across an important point. And what was the point? Jesus' family is an open circle, not a closed one.

The church is a family, but an ever-expanding one. We should never assume that family means "just us." It is not a tight circle. It is not exclusive or elite. This *family,* as Jesus defined it, is always open, always receiving, always accepting, and always growing.

There is something else to be said about this imagery. David Kinnaman, in his book *You Lost Me,* discusses some of the ways the church can be more helpful and responsive to people in the twenty-first century. In one section he says this:

> The Christian community [that is, the church] is one of the few places on earth where those who represent the full scope of human life, literally from the cradle to the grave, come together with a singular motive and mission. The church is (or should be) a place of racial, gender, socioeconomic, and cultural reconciliation— because Jesus commanded that our love would be the telltale sign of our devotion to him (see John 13:35)—as well as a community where various age demographics genuinely love each other and work together with unity and respect....
> I believe we are called to connect our past (traditions

and elders) with our future (the next generation). Christians are members of a living organism called the church.... If you are a younger Christian, pursue wisdom from older believers. I want to really emphasize the idea of *pursuing* wisdom. One of the overriding themes of Proverbs is that wisdom is elusive. It's like love. It seems obvious and easy at first but then turns out to require patience and long-term commitment. Likewise, finding a wise and trustworthy mentor doesn't happen by accident. Knock on doors, send emails, make calls....

If you are [an older Christian], I encourage you to come to grips with the revolutionary nature of [younger Christians'] cultural moment. Young Christians are living through a period of unprecedented social and technological change, compressed in an astounding manner, and the longer we take to acknowledge and respond to these changes, the more we allow the disconnection between generations to progress. Ask yourself how available you have been to younger Christians. The generation gap is growing, fueled in part by technology, so it takes extra effort to be on the same page.... Start conversations in your community that lead to reconciliation between generations and fearless disciples of every age.[15]

Kinnaman suggests that we see the church as "a partnership of generations fulfilling God's purposes in their time."[16] In other words, a family, yes, but a family with a purpose, a cause, and a calling. A family that encompasses every age group and incorporates, as Jesus said, "Anyone who does the will of [our] Father in heaven!"

May it be so for you. May you experience the rich intergenerational family of faith that is the church. May you fulfill the calling of "a chosen generation,"[17] "a community where various age demographics genuinely love each other and work together with unity and respect."[18]

"WORSHIP IS A UNIVERSAL URGE, HARD-WIRED BY GOD INTO THE VERY FIBER OF OUR BEING—AN INBUILT NEED TO CONNECT WITH GOD."
—RICK WARREN

CHAPTER 5

CONNECT

You sit in a folding beach chair and watch the sunrise over the ocean.

Brilliant rays of light color the horizon. The sound of gentle waves lapping the sand delights you as the cold ocean water washes over your toes. A breeze caresses your cheek. You inhale the fresh salty air.

Moment by moment the scene shifts and changes. The sun bursts into sight. Seagulls dip and call. Waves crest and roll away. Your heart fills. Your mouth opens. You feel like singing. You feel like saying, "Thank you." You feel like worshiping.

Chances are, you've been there, or somewhere like it.

Maybe it wasn't on a beach at sunrise. Possibly it was on a woodland path or beside a thundering waterfall. Or it might have been in a maternity ward as a new life entered this world. Perhaps it was a moment when you were surprised by an anonymous kindness or overwhelming generosity. Could've been after your first bite of a perfectly prepared meal. Whenever and wherever it happened, in that moment, you felt a surge of something wonderful—emotion, joy, gratitude, and worship.

No matter where you are in your spiritual journey, you have a need to worship. You have felt drawn upward. You have longed to experience the supernatural, to connect with God, to respond to the transcendent. It is a universal human need. We may try to deny it, but we cannot escape it.

In his landmark book, *The Purpose-Driven Life,* Rick Warren writes,

> Anthropologists have noted that worship is a universal urge, hard-wired by God into the very fiber of our being—an inbuilt need to connect with God. Worship is as natural as eating or breathing. If we fail

to worship God, we always find a substitute, even if it ends up being ourselves.[1]

Most people sense this keenly, and express it in one way or another. We may not be sure what we believe, but we talk about being "spiritual." We want to experience the sublime. We want to know God and feel a connection with Him. We also sense that there are benefits to be enjoyed when we do so.

Church Helps You Experience the Benefits of Worship

One of the reasons the church exists is to help you fulfill your innate, God-given need to worship. The Bible describes the very first church in its earliest days like this:

> They followed a daily discipline of worship in the Temple followed by meals at home, every meal a celebration, exuberant and joyful, as they praised God.[2]

They worshiped in the temple (at that time, everyone in the church was Jewish, so it only made sense). They worshiped in their homes. They worshiped around the table. They worshiped as a way of life, "exuberant and joyful," praising God.

Everyone needs that. Every human soul is wired to worship. And while the weekend worship gatherings of the church are not intended to be the only time and place you worship (remember, those first Christians worshiped at home, too), they provide an introduction to the many blessings of worship.

Worship reorients the mind, heart, and life. One day, when Isaiah was worshiping in the temple, he received a vision and heard God's voice in a way that scared him, changed him, and took his life in a new direction.[3] True worship will often do that. It will remind you who God is, and who you are. It will change you and point your steps in new directions. It will focus you on what is truly important. It will turn you around, and may even turn you into someone you never imagined you could be.

Worship chases away fear, doubt, worry, and selfishness. Brian, a fifty-five-year-old father of three, says, "I can't begin to count the number of times I have entered church tired and discouraged and even depressed. There have been times I honestly didn't want to be there, and I didn't know how I would overcome my rotten mood enough to worship. But I can honestly say, I've never left a worship service the same way I went in. I may still have had the same problems and challenges, but worship has never failed to lift my burdens and calm my fears." The Bible says that King Saul, the first king of ancient Israel, was tormented by anxiety and depression. But when David, a true worshiper of God who served in Saul's court, played and sang for the king, Saul would find relief.[4]

Worship provides an outlet for gratitude. English painter and poet Dante Gabriel Rossetti famously said that the worst moment for the atheist is when he is really thankful and has nobody to thank.[5] One of the great blessings of worship is providing an outlet for the gratitude that often wells up in the human heart.

Worship attunes your heart to the voice of God. Many people wish that they could hear from God and receive His direction in an important decision or at a critical crossroads, but they don't know how. The ears of their hearts, so to speak, aren't accustomed to hearing God, so even if He does speak they may not hear. But one of the blessings of regular worship is that it attunes the worshiper's heart to the voice of God—like the young boy, Samuel, who lived and slept "in the house of the LORD."[6] When God called out to Samuel, he was in God's house, he was available, and with the help of Eli the priest, he soon recognized and obeyed God's voice.

Worship opens the door to the supernatural. Do you long to see God work? Do you want to experience miracles? Do you hope for healing? Do you need deliverance? Then worship! When God's people, the nation of Israel, prepared to cross into the Promised Land, they placed the worship leaders—the priests and the ark of the covenant—at the head of the procession, and the Jordan River parted for them.[7] Years later, when a vast army of Moabites and Ammonites attacked God's people, "[King] Jehoshaphat appointed men to sing to the Lord and to praise him for the splendor of his holiness as they went out at the head of the army, saying: 'Give thanks to the Lord, for his love endures forever.' As they began to sing and praise, the Lord set ambushes against the men of Ammon and Moab and Mount Seir who were invading Judah, and they were defeated."[8]

Worship sows seeds of joy in your life. Rick Warren writes,

> An amazing thing happens when we offer praise and thanksgiving to God. When we give God enjoyment, our own hearts are filled with joy!
>
> My mother loved to cook for me. Even after I married Kay, when we would visit my parents, Mom prepared incredible home-cooked feasts. One of her great pleasures in life was watching us kids eat and enjoy what she prepared. The more we enjoyed eating it, the more enjoyment it gave her.
>
> But we also enjoyed pleasing Mom by expressing our enjoyment of her meal. It worked both ways. As I would eat the great meal, I would rave about it and praise my mother. I intended not only to enjoy the food, but to please my mother. Everyone was happy.
>
> Worship works both ways, too. We enjoy what God has done for us, and when we express that enjoyment to God, it brings him joy—but it also increases our joy. The book of Psalms says, "The righteous are glad and rejoice in his presence; they are happy and shout for joy."[9]

Worship promotes unity with the global and historical church. When you participate in public worship, you are uniting with countless others—black and white, Asian and Latino, male and female, young and old, single and married, rich and poor, broken and burdened, suit-wearing and sari-clad, in the tropics and in the tundra, and with the martyrs and saints of twenty centuries—to say that God is worthy to receive "power and wealth and wisdom and strength and honor and glory and praise!"[10]

Those seven blessings of worship are not exhaustive. They merely scratch the surface. But for most people, church is the first—and most frequent—place where those blessings and many other benefits of worship can be found.

Church Can Train You to Worship Better

True worship does not happen automatically. In fact, while worship is instinctive and natural to the human heart, it is not only possible but necessary to learn *how* to worship *and* to learn how to worship better, how to make it more pleasing to God and more beneficial to you and to others.

For example, Psalm 95 says this:

> Come, let us sing for joy to the LORD;
> let us shout aloud to the Rock of our salvation.
> Let us come before him with thanksgiving
> and extol him with music and song.[11]

And verse six of that psalm says,

> Come, let us bow down in worship,
> let us kneel before the LORD our Maker.[12]

Those are nice sentiments, right? But here's the thing. If you've never been to church before—or have participated only rarely—you may not know the words or melody to the songs. You may not feel comfortable bowing or kneeling. And you are definitely not going to shout.

Besides, everyone has their own style, and some churches are more formal than others, more traditional than others, more expressive than others, and so on. And that's a good thing. Diversity is not necessarily disunity; in the church as in Creation, God delights in different colors, sounds, and styles.

But worshiping regularly with others in church breaks down barriers and gives training, not only in worship *styles* but also in worship *skills*. As you gather with others, you will become more and more comfortable singing your praises to God, as the Bible tells us to do—even if you can't carry a tune. Over time, you will get better at consciously and actively *praying* the words of a song as you sing. You may even become adept at *personalizing* the words so they reflect what you are feeling at that particular moment.

You may never want to pray aloud in public, and that's okay. However, by gathering with others to worship, you will hear people pray. You may be awed at the simplicity and beauty of one person's prayers and irritated by the pomposity of someone else's prayers, but as you listen (and pray along silently), you will learn—little by little—a few things about prayer that can be applied to your own spiritual life.

Someday you may notice the lady across the room who cups her hands sometimes while she sings, as if she's saying, "Lord, I'm ready to receive whatever you have to give me today." Or you may realize that the teenager whom you thought was drawing pictures during the sermon is actually taking notes. And you may sooner or later decide to try something like that yourself, or not. Either way, you've still learned something, haven't you?

As the preacher speaks, if you pay attention and follow along, you may find yourself learning how to read and understand the Bible, and possibly study it for yourself. When people give testimonies of how God is working in their lives, you might gain some tips for how to explain your faith to others. As you see how different people contribute to the worship experience, you might be surprised to feel an interest in serving in similar ways yourself.

The "training ground" of public worship will not only help you develop skills to use in corporate times of worship, it will also train you to sing, pray, read, study, and connect to God at other times as well. The songs you learn will become a part of your worship language; you may find yourself singing as you drive or as you shower. Prayer will become a more frequent part of your life. The Bible will be more accessible to you. Practices that once impressed or confused you will become skills that help you worship God throughout all your life.

Church Can Empower and Enrich Your Worship Life

Few people in history have worshiped like David, the second king of Israel. He danced in worship as the Ark of the Covenant returned to Jerusalem. He wrote worship songs. He trained and organized the worship leaders of ancient Israel. The Bible even describes him as "a man after [God's] own heart."[13] If anyone knew how to worship, it was David.

He worshiped in the morning:

> Listen to my voice in the morning, Lord.
>   Each morning I bring my requests to you and wait expectantly.[14]

He worshiped at night:

> On my bed I remember you;
>   I think of you through the watches of the night.
> Because you are my help,
>   I sing in the shadow of your wings.[15]

He worshiped in palaces and in caves. He worshiped when he felt good and when he felt awful. He worshiped in kingly robes and in his linen underwear. He may well have had the most fulfilling and intimate private worship life ever. Yet, for all his ability and enthusiasm for worshiping God personally and privately, he also joined in corporate worship experiences:

> I will worship at your Temple with deepest awe.[16]

> I will proclaim your name to my brothers and sisters.
>   I will praise you among your assembled people....
> I will praise you in the great assembly.
>   I will fulfill my vows in the presence of those who worship you.[17]

> With all my heart
> I will thank the Lord
> when his people meet.[18]

If anyone could have said, "I can worship God anywhere," you would think it would have been David, right? If anyone could have claimed, "I don't need 'church,'" David could. But he didn't. Which prompts the question: Why? We don't have to wonder because he answers that question repeatedly:

Lord, I love the house where you live,
the place where your glory dwells.[19]

One thing I ask from the Lord,
this only do I seek:
that I may dwell in the house of the Lord
all the days of my life,
to gaze on the beauty of the Lord
and to seek him in his temple.
For in the day of trouble
he will keep me safe in his dwelling;
he will hide me in the shelter of his sacred tent
and set me high upon a rock.[20]

Now this I know:
    The Lord gives victory to his anointed.
He answers him from his heavenly sanctuary
with the victorious power of his right hand.[21]

David found a power and energy in corporate worship that thrilled his soul and instilled in him a love for the house of God. He spoke and sang as though he encountered God's glory in the temple in a special way. He experienced a safety and shelter there that he didn't find elsewhere. He found a heightened level of power and victory and encouragement and hope in corporate worship.

It can be a wonderful blessing to sing a song like, "How Great Thou Art" or "You Never Let Go" in a private and personal time of worship. Such moments are indispensable to your spiritual health and growth. But it is a different experience—and just as indispensable—to sing those words in unison with others. Whether you're uniting your voice with fifty others or five thousand, something powerful happens when you join forces with others to worship "the Lord God Almighty, who was, who is, and who is to come."[22]

Likewise, attending worship with others presents opportunities you simply can't enjoy in private worship. "Not long ago, a young woman in my church gave a short testimony of some of the things God has been doing in her life," said Hope, a mother of four. "I couldn't believe how God spoke to me through her. Her words washed over me like water and filled me up in ways I can't describe. It was a huge answer to prayer." God might use a short hug or a warm greeting from someone to bless you. You might learn of a concert or a service opportunity that you wouldn't have known about if you hadn't been in church that week. And you might be led in creative acts of worship and giving to God that would never have occurred to you if you hadn't praised God "among [his] assembled people."

Brian Tome, senior pastor of Crossroads Community Church in Cincinnati, Ohio, describes one of his most memorable worship experiences:

> Years ago, we challenged the notion that people didn't want to be engaged and pushed in a weekend service. We gave everybody Sharpies and ornamental glass bulbs and told people to write what their idol was on them. Then as a sign of dying to yourself and dying to your idol, we asked people to come forward and smash them in wooden coffins.
>
> I'll never forget people throwing their symbolic idols into coffins. Some of the bulbs didn't break as the glass was piling up and yet, people would reach their hand into shards of glass to retrieve their bulb and smash it again. It was a defining moment for people as they walked away from their idol and died to self. It was also a defining moment for our church when we realized that the days were over when we couldn't push people and tacitly engage them.[23]

Don Wilson, the senior pastor of Christ's Church of the Valley in Peoria, Arizona, said, "One week I asked everyone at the close of the service to leave their shoes on stage and told them we would be sending the shoes to people in poorer countries that couldn't afford them. The response was so positive that many of the parents asked us to do the same thing in our youth and children's ministry the next week."[24]

Imagine what it was like to be a worshiper that weekend and not only give away your own shoes, but watch a stream of people do the same. Imagine seeing a mountain of shoes left at the front of that church auditorium. Picture walking barefoot to your car...and seeing your friends and neighbors doing the same. Envision your shoes and their shoes being worn by people half a world away who would otherwise have no shoes at all.

Another pastor, Steve Stroope, recalled a twenty-fifth anniversary service of Lake Pointe Church in Rockwall, Texas: "We invited everyone who had been saved at Lake Pointe to come to the front and light a candle during a worship song. There were as many people at the front holding candles as there were standing at their seats."[25] What a moving moment that must have been, to see so many changed lives represented by those lights. Imagine, too, if you had not only attended but also given to that church in money and service over the years, how it would have blessed your heart to see such a graphic depiction of your church's ministry and the impact of your gifts.

A month after Robin's granddaughter, Calleigh, was born, the family learned that she had cystic fibrosis. She and her husband, and their daughter and son-in-law, cried together and prayed together often in the first few weeks after they learned of the physical challenges Calleigh would face in the years to come. They each prayed separately, too, remembering Calleigh in their personal times of worship. "But I can't even begin to describe what it was like, a few weeks later, to see our daughter holding her baby at the front of our church auditorium while our pastors and church family surrounded us all and prayed for Calleigh, and for us. Even now, it brings tears to my eyes to talk about it. It was a moment I don't think I'll ever forget."

Those are the kinds of empowering and enriching experiences that come only to those who make it a habit to connect with God and "thank the Lord when his people meet," as David sang.[26]

Your soul is wired for worship. And worship should not

be confined to just a couple hours on a weekend. In order to meet your soul's need, worship needs to infiltrate and permeate all of your life—"your everyday, ordinary life—your sleeping, eating, going-to-work, and walking-around life."[27] However, corporate worship is a crucial ingredient of your worship life, too, because church can help you experience the benefits of worship, train you to worship better, and empower and enrich your worship life.

"WE KNOW NOTHING
FOR CERTAIN, BUT WE SEEM
TO SEE THAT THE WORLD
TURNS UPON GROWING,
GROWS TOWARD GROWING,
AND GROWING GREEN
AND CLEAN."
—ANNIE DILLARD

CHAPTER 6

IMPROVE

When you were an infant, your brain was one-fourth the size it is now. In your first year of life, however, your brain reached 70 percent of its eventual size—and 85 percent by age three. You didn't plan that rapid growth. You didn't strategize to significantly expand your brain between your first "goos" and "gagas." You didn't even know you were growing, though you've never grown so much and so quickly since. You grew, nonetheless, because growth and improvement was hard-wired into your DNA. It is part of the human condition. The drive to thrive, the "groove to improve," is part and parcel of your makeup.

It can be denied, of course. It can be neglected. It can even be lost. But the chances are high that if you're still reading this book, you possess a hefty helping of "yearning for learning." Pulitzer-winner Annie Dillard wrote, "We know nothing for certain, but we seem to see that the world turns upon growing, grows toward growing, and growing green and clean."[1]

No kidding. Just take a look at the dandelions on your lawn, the zucchini in your garden, or the dust bunnies under your bed. Of course, for you, personally, that urge to grow and improve may have been strongest in your early childhood—people who study such things say children develop 85 percent of their intellect, personality, and skills by age five[2]—and some of us, it seems, haven't learned much of anything since then. Others still want to grow, learn, develop, and improve, though. There are things you long to figure out. Ways you want to progress. Expand, even. Deepen. Broaden. Heighten.

And one of the reasons the church exists is to help you do that—in multiple ways.

Church Can Help You Grow Spiritually

It may seem too obvious to say that church can help you grow spiritually. Who doesn't know that, right? But that doesn't mean it is automatic. Some people have absorbed or developed an attitude toward church involvement as basically discharging an obligation. For them it's not about learning, growing, and improving, but about getting a moral obligation out of the way (or getting Mom off your back). Others figure that all the activities of the church equate to little more than periodically bathing with a wet wipe. You show up, put in your time, and God more or less pats you on the head and sends you on your way, until you need to wash off the grit and grime of real life again.

Those ideas bear no similarity to what Jesus said and what the Bible teaches, though. For example, just a quick look at the themes of the letters to the churches in the Bible reveal that one of the purposes of the church is to help you grow, learn, develop, and improve as a person and as a follower of Jesus:

- Romans: "Grasp what it means to be justified by faith in Jesus"
- 1 Corinthians: "Here's how to conduct yourself as a follower of Jesus"
- 2 Corinthians: "Learn to be gracious, forgiving, and generous"
- Galatians: "Reject legalism and enjoy your freedom in Christ"
- Ephesians: "Enjoy your position, privilege, and purpose in Christ"
- Philippians: "Rejoice always"
- Colossians: "Don't fall for falsehood; you're better than that"
- 1 Thessalonians: "Live today in light of what is ahead"
- 2 Thessalonians: "You are chosen and called, which should affect your conduct"

Those are oversimplifications, of course; each of those letters (written to actual people, real churches, in specific places) is much richer and deeper than those summaries, but you get the idea. From the very beginning, the idea of church was that it would make a difference in people's lives and help participants improve in any number of ways: becoming more like Jesus, more functional in their lives, more valuable to their communities, and more influential in the world.

The same is true today. Your church is not responsible for your development; you are. But your church can make a huge difference in your spiritual vitality, growth, and satisfaction. Here are three specific ways church involvement can do that.

Church can equip you with the key skills necessary for spiritual growth. Church attendance doesn't automatically bring about spiritual growth.[3] But regular involvement in a church can expose you to and equip you with the skills that produce spiritual growth: prayer, how to read and understand your Bible, how to use your gifts in serving God, and how to comfortably and effectively share your faith with others. While you may have first learned to pray at your mother's knee, chances are good that there is room for improvement. After all, even Jesus' first disciples—who as adult Jewish males had been praying many times a day since they were children—once approached Him with the plea, "Lord, teach us to pray."[4] And, as mentioned previously, the educated Ethiopian who met Philip on the Gaza road could obviously read the words of Scripture, but the church—in the person of Philip—helped him gain a better understanding that led to a deeper commitment.[5] Also, though Timothy had a lot of experience traveling and working beside Paul, the apostle nonetheless instructed his protégé, "Fan into flames the spiritual gift God gave you when I laid my hands on you. For God has not given us a spirit of fear and timidity, but of power, love, and self-discipline. So never be ashamed to tell others about our Lord."[6] As Jesus, Philip, and Paul continued to teach the first wave of Christians, so the church exists today to help you develop and improve the skills that will contribute to your ongoing spiritual vitality, growth, and satisfaction.

Church can help you become mature enough to feed yourself. When a person first experiences new life through faith in Jesus Christ and begins intentionally following Him, it is natural and good for that person to ravenously desire the kind of teaching described in the paragraph above. In fact, the apostle Peter wrote,

Like newborn babies, you must crave pure spiritual milk so that you will grow into a full experience of salvation. Cry out for this nourishment, now that you have had a taste of the Lord's kindness.[7]

But the purpose of "spiritual milk" is "so that you will grow," as Peter said; it is to sustain the infant Christian until he or she can learn to handle solid food and feed himself or herself. The purpose of your church is not to give you a weekly spoon-feeding, but to teach you skills for spiritual growth and equip you to feed yourself in prayer, Bible reading, Bible study, service, and intentional, purposeful relationships with others.

Church can help you identify next steps for growth and challenge you to take them. In recent years, hundreds of thousands of people have gleefully participated in IRONMAN triathlons, Spartan Races, and Tough Mudder competitions. People actually pay money—more than a hundred dollars—to endure an obstacle course designed to tax their physical strength and stamina, and assault their emotional and mental well-being. Why do they do it? For the challenge, accomplishment, and the satisfaction of pushing themselves beyond what they've ever accomplished before. Thirty-five-year-old Bill, who has participated in three Tough Mudder challenges, said, "I do it to prove to myself that I can finish and endure such miserable conditions. There is a huge sense of accomplishment because only 70 percent of those who start manage to finish the race—and I have always had a hard time 'finishing' things in life. So to be able to go out there and push myself to the limit and survive—and finish—makes me feel like I can do almost anything."

A good church can do that, too, believe it or not. It can show you helpful next steps toward spiritual maturity. Through teaching, training, and the example or influence of others who are pursuing the same goals as you, involvement in a healthy church can push you toward a place you might never have thought you could go. It can also give you people to celebrate with you when you get there!

Church Can Teach You Practical Skills

This was touched on briefly in chapter four, however, it bears not only repeating, but also amplification because churches today offer a wide and varied array of classes, courses, and coaches for the development of practical, valuable skills.

Travis, for example, became involved in church because his older brothers started playing volleyball in the church gymnasium and he had tagged along. Almost immediately, one of the other guys on the volleyball court named Brad invited Travis to church.

When he first began attending church with Brad, Travis was a shy—backward, even—fifteen-year-old. He smoked heavily, like his older brothers. When Brad introduced him to others, Travis hung his head, shook hands weakly, and mumbled an awkward hello. Soon, however, with Brad's encouragement, Travis gained confidence—and a few skills. He learned not only to look others in the eyes, but to offer a firm handshake and a reasonably warm greeting as well.

That doesn't seem like much, right? It was only the beginning. With Brad's encouragement, Travis soon got his first paying job. Around the same time, their church offered a six-week seminar on money management, so Brad and Travis completed the seminar together.

With advice from some of the men in the church, Travis started a small computer business while still in high school. He also applied to several colleges in the area. Though he struggled at first, his church not only helped him with a couple of scholarships, but also helped him find an internship that fulfilled his graduation requirements.

Travis commuted from home and maintained his computer business through college, which enabled him to graduate with no student debt (and, thanks to the financial seminar he and Brad had taken years earlier, he avoided all other debt as well). At the age of twenty-three, Travis was a college graduate, debt-free, and owned his own business. That's when he began dating Cheri.

As their relationship got more serious, Travis and Cheri started premarital counseling sessions with Josh and Julie, one of the married couples in the church. By the time they finished the premarital counseling process, however, neither Travis nor Cheri thought they should pursue marriage, so they broke up. It was hard and hurtful, but might have been much worse without Josh and Julie's help and support.

Travis was still hurting from the breakup with Cheri when he enrolled in a Bible study at church on healing from life's losses. In the course of that study, he realized that so many of his fellow church members were dealing with tragic circumstances—divorce, job loss, even the death of a child—and he also met Jessica, a single mother whose infant daughter had been born with a genetic condition that presented numerous challenges.

Soon, Travis and Jessica were dating. Shortly after that, they commenced premarital counseling with Josh and Julie, and six months after the end of the Bible study on healing from life's losses, they were married—and Cheri even attended the wedding.

Just ten years after he became involved in that church, Travis' life had been indescribably enriched by the church. Spiritually, of course, but also by the fundamental interpersonal skills he learned early on from Brad and others—financially, vocationally, educationally, and relationally. In fact, Travis and Brad, and their wives, were recently asked by their pastor to join a training group for small-group leaders. The pastor wants them to start a small group to teach principles, swap skills, and encourage young couples in the task of raising children and building strong families.

Travis' story could be repeated thousands of times in church after church. Church-sponsored classes, courses, and coaches can help you get out of debt and manage your finances; prepare for marriage or repair your marriage; learn parenting skills or help you care for aging parents; become a better employee, a better leader, a better student, or a better teacher; build a God-honoring business, and more.

Church Can Offer You Crucial Support

When you look at the Bible and study the early church, you will see people who endured things we can't even relate to. People were thrown in jail for being Christ-followers. They were physically attacked. There were contracts put out on their lives. There is one such story in Acts 12. It starts out like this:

> It was about this time that King Herod arrested some who belonged to the church, intending to persecute them. He had James, the brother of John, put to death with the sword. When he saw that this pleased the Jews, he proceeded to seize Peter also. This happened during the Feast of Unleavened Bread. After arresting him, he put him in prison, handing him over to be guarded by four squads of four soldiers each. Herod intended to bring him out for public trial after the Passover.
>
> So Peter was kept in prison, but the church was earnestly praying to God for him.
>
> The night before Herod was to bring him to trial, Peter was sleeping between two soldiers, bound with two chains, and sentries stood guard at the entrance.[8]

It is important to grasp how serious Peter's situation was. King Herod was not a nice man; he had already beheaded James, the brother of John, and that was just the latest atrocity the church had endured. Stephen had been stoned, Paul had to sneak out of Damascus under cover of night, and now it looked like Peter was going to be next.

And yet, notice this: Peter was in lockup, he was chained between two soldiers, it was looking like he'd be executed the next day, and...what was he doing? Was he freaking out? Was he pacing back and forth? Demanding to see his lawyer?

No. He was sleeping. That is truly amazing. He doesn't seem to be overwrought.

The story continues:

> Suddenly an angel of the Lord appeared and a light shone in the cell. He struck Peter on the side and woke him up. "Quick, get up!" he said, and the chains fell off Peter's wrists.

Then the angel said to him, "Put on your clothes and sandals." And Peter did so. "Wrap your cloak around you and follow me," the angel told him. Peter followed him out of the prison, but he had no idea that what the angel was doing was really happening; he thought he was seeing a vision.

They passed the first and second guards and came to the iron gate leading to the city. It opened for them by itself, and they went through it. When they had walked the length of one street, suddenly the angel left him.

Then Peter came to himself and said, "Now I know without a doubt that the Lord sent his angel and rescued me from Herod's clutches and from everything the Jewish people were anticipating."

When this had dawned on him, he went to the house of Mary the mother of John, also called Mark, where many people had gathered and were praying. Peter knocked at the outer entrance, and a servant girl named Rhoda came to answer the door. When she recognized Peter's voice, she was so overjoyed she ran back without opening it and exclaimed, "Peter is at the door!"

"You're out of your mind," they told her. When she kept insisting that it was so, they said, "It must be his angel."

But Peter kept on knocking.[9]

This is one of the funniest scenes in the Bible. Peter has just been sprung from prison—by an angel, no less—and when he goes to the house where the church is gathered to pray for him, the girl who answers forgets to open the door! She leaves the poor guy standing there while she goes inside and says, "You won't believe who's at the door!" And the account concludes,

> But Peter kept on knocking, and when they opened the door and saw him, they were astonished. Peter motioned with his hand for them to be quiet and

described how the Lord had brought him out of prison. "Tell James and the brothers about this," he said, and then he left for another place.[10]

This is an early account of how the church supports those who are in difficulty. You may not be chained to soldiers in a Roman prison, but you may feel confined by a job, beat down by your bills, trapped in a situation, imprisoned by a sickness, or chained to some burden, but notice what the church did for Peter, because it can do the same for you.

The church can surround you with prayer. Remember verse 5? "So Peter was kept in prison, but the church was earnestly praying to God for him."[11] If you're going through difficult times, having a church family to support you in prayer can be a huge advantage. You have a built-in prayer support system when tough times hit. Some churches activate a prayer chain when someone is hurting and makes it known; some prayer chains even reach around the world. Your pastor and church leaders can gather around you for prayer, and may agree to pray for you and with you on a daily basis.

The church can help you hear what God is saying. Remember Peter in the prison? The angel woke him up; he didn't ask the angel questions, he wasn't trying to figure out what was going on. He seemed to be more or less in shock, and just did what the angel told him to do. When you're going through tough times, the church can help you keep an eye out for angels, or chains falling off, or doors opening, or doors closing.

The church can help you see God's hand in your challenges. Once the angel guided Peter out of the prison and into the fresh night air, he awoke to the reality of his situation. He said, "Now I know without a doubt that the Lord sent his angel and rescued me."[12] The tragedy is, when bad things happen and we're in difficult times, we tend to turn the wrong direction. We turn to anger: "How could God let this happen?" We turn to self-pity: "Why does my life have to be so hard?" We turn to discouragement: "Oh, forget it! It's not worth the effort!" However, the church can help you turn to God and see His hand, His purpose, and His plan in what is happening.

The church can open doors for you. It took a little patience in Peter's case, but the church eventually got around to opening the door for Peter. The same can be true for you. Doors may open through prayer, study, or relationships. The church may open a door to treatment or recovery. The church may open a door by introducing you to new opportunities or training you in new skills. Just two days before this chapter was written, in fact, the following conversation took place in the moments before a church service between Ian, a man who had recently lost his job, and his friend Jack:

Jack: "How have things been going? Any movement on the job front?"

Ian: "I have to tell you—I went to my first meeting of a new small group last Wednesday."

Jack: "How was it?"

Ian: "It was a God thing. We went around and introduced ourselves, and when my turn came, I went ahead and told them I had lost my job and was in crisis."

Jack: "Good for you!"

Ian: "Wait, that's not the best part. As soon as I finished, the woman next to me told me she worked in human resources—for a company in my field! She gave me her card and said to send her my résumé."

Jack: "Wow."

Ian: "I know. Even if she doesn't end up offering me a job, it was exactly what I needed at the time."

Some doors open through relationships, while other doors open as the result of more purposeful planning, like job fairs or church directories. Some churches offer writer's groups, men's groups, women's groups, parenting groups, recovery groups (for those struggling with addictions, depression, grief, etc.), and all kinds of support groups (for parents navigating the adoption process, single parents, couples struggling with infertility, those who are recently widowed, and so on).

The church can persevere and celebrate with you. Once the church opened the door and let Peter in, the Bible says he had to quiet them down in order to describe the Lord's deliverance.

And then the Bible says he told them to share the good news of his release with others in the church.[13] That, too, was a part of the church's ministry of support. It is a blessing not only to have people who will persevere with you and help you through your struggles, but it brings great joy to have people who will mark your progress and celebrate with you.

The Bible tells us to "rejoice with those who rejoice, and mourn with those who mourn."[14] Sadly, too many people lack that resource; their daughter gets engaged, and they find themselves shopping around for a church or pastor or justice of the peace to host and perform the wedding. Or they face a loss or a challenge and they have no support system to keep them from crashing to the ground.

May it not be so for you. Instead, may you find the kind of support described by Bill Hybels in his book, *Courageous Leadership:*

> I had just finished presenting my weekend message... and I was standing [up front]. A young married couple approached me, placed a blanketed bundle in my arms, and asked me to pray for their baby.
>
> As I asked what the baby's name was, the mother pulled back the blanket that had covered the infant's face. I felt my knees begin to buckle. I thought I was going to faint.... In my arms was the most horribly deformed baby I had ever seen....
>
> All I could say was, "Oh my...oh my...oh my."
>
> "Her name is Emily," said the mother.
>
> "We've been told she has about six weeks to live," added the father. "We would like you to pray that before she dies she will know and feel our love."
>
> Barely able to mouth the words, I whispered, "Let's pray." Together we prayed for Emily. Oh, did we pray. As I handed her back to her parents, I asked, "Is there anything we can do for you, any way that we as a church can serve you during this time?"
>
> The father responded... "Bill, we're okay. Really we are. We've been in a loving small group for years. Our group members knew that this pregnancy had

complications. They were at our house the night we learned the news, and they were at the hospital when Emily was delivered. They helped us absorb the reality of the whole thing. They even cleaned our house and fixed our meals when we brought her home. They pray for us constantly and call us several times a day. They are even helping us plan Emily's funeral."

Just then the three other couples stepped forward and surrounded Emily and her parents....

It was a picture I will carry to my grave.[15]

Everyone goes through difficult times. You can't avoid them. However, you can endure them, by God's grace and with God's help through God's church.

"THERE IS WOVEN INSIDE EACH OF US A DESIRE FOR SOMETHING MORE—A CRAVING TO BE PART OF SOMETHING BIGGER, GREATER, AND MORE PROFOUND THAN OUR RELATIVELY MEANINGLESS DAY-BY-DAY EXISTENCE."

—PAUL DAVID TRIPP

CHAPTER 7

IMPACT

Author and pastor Max Lucado offers a parable in his book, *Outlive Your Life.*

He describes a ship encountering a series of uncharted islands in the South Seas. At one island after another, the ship's captain and crew encounter sadness. "Underfed children. Tribes in conflict. No farming or food development, no treatment for the sick, and no schools."[1] It is a dispiriting experience.

But the ship soon discovers another island, and this one is different—gloriously so. Health. Food. Roads. Beauty. Happiness. When the ship's captain asks the island's chief why this place is so different from the others, the chief answers with two words: "Father Benjamin." So the captain asks, "Can you take me to see him?"

No one could tell the story better than Lucado:

> The chief nods and signals for two tribesmen to join him. They guide the captain over a jungle ridge to a simple, expansive medical clinic. It is equipped with clean beds and staffed with trained caretakers. They show the captain the shelves of medicine and introduce him to the staff. The captain, though impressed, sees nothing of Father Benjamin. He repeats his request. "I would like to see Father Benjamin. Can you take me to where he lives?"
>
> The three natives look puzzled. They confer among themselves. After several minutes the chief invites, "Follow us to the other side of the island." They walk along the shoreline until they reach a series of fishponds. Canals connect the ponds to the ocean. As the tide rises, fish pass from the ocean into the

ponds. The islanders then lower canal gates and trap the fish for harvest.

Again the captain is amazed. He meets fishermen and workers, gatekeepers and net casters. But he sees nothing of Father Benjamin. He wonders if he is making himself clear.

"I don't see Father Benjamin. Please take me to where he lives."

The trio talks alone again. After some discussion the chief offers, "Let's go up the mountain." They lead the captain up a steep, narrow path. After many twists and turns the path deposits them in front of a grass-roofed chapel. The voice of the chief is soft and earnest. "He has taught us about God."

He escorts the captain inside and shows him the altar, a large wooden cross, several rows of benches, and a Bible.

"Is this where Father Benjamin lives?" the captain asks.

The men nod and smile.

"May I talk to him?"

Their faces grow suddenly serious. "Oh, that would be impossible."

"Why?"

"He died many years ago."

The bewildered captain stares at the men. "I asked to see him, and you showed me a clinic, some fish farms, and this chapel. You said nothing of his death."

"You didn't ask about his death," the chief explains. "You asked to see where he lives. We showed you."[2]

Everyone wants to be "Father Benjamin." We all need to be useful. We long to have an impact on others. We want to know our lives make a difference. This is a fundamental human need—so much so, in fact, that we can't feel true and lasting happiness without it.

Church Can Help You Be a Part of Something Bigger Than You

Author and speaker Paul David Tripp says,

> There is woven inside each of us a desire for something more—a craving to be part of something bigger, greater, and more profound than our relatively meaningless day-by-day existence... We simply weren't constructed to live only for ourselves. We were placed on earth to be part of something bigger than the narrow borders of our own survival and our own little definition of happiness.[3]

You may have tasted the sensation of being part of something bigger than yourself in a football stadium as seventy-thousand voices joined yours in cheering your team's touchdown, your team's heroics, your team's victory. Or you may have felt that way when—after weeks and months of stapling papers, sealing envelopes, distributing pamphlets, and calling voters—your chosen candidate is elected to office. Perhaps it happened in a school ceremony, as you marched to a stage in front of hundreds—even thousands—as the latest in a long line of graduates from a venerated institution, a line that has included poets and pundits, prime ministers and presidents!

Those are heady experiences. And they give a taste of what it is like to be part of something bigger than yourself. Yet, those moments provide only a taste of what your heart really longs for, what your soul craves. What you really want is impact. You don't want to just *cheer* the players on the field, you want to *be* one of them; you don't want to merely celebrate the score, you want to score.

On the day the church was born, people from all over the world had gathered for a major festival. They had come to worship at the magnificent temple Herod had built in Jerusalem. They were Parthians, Medes, and Elamites from Mesopotamia, Judea, Cappadocia, Pontus and Asia, Phrygia and Pamphylia, Egypt and Libya and Rome—nearly every part of the known world at that time.

As mentioned in the beginning of the book, that diverse, multiracial, multilingual crowd packed the streets of Jerusalem when God's Holy Spirit descended on a tiny church in an upstairs room on a major thoroughfare. Suddenly, the Galilean Jews in that room began speaking—loudly—in new languages. Languages they had never learned, but which people in the street recognized as their native language.

We don't know just when those followers of Jesus spilled out of the room where they were meeting, but they did, and soon Peter was preaching to a vast crowd, explaining what was happening. It was the fulfillment of prophecy, he said. It was the pouring out of God's Spirit. It was the day of salvation. It was God's kingdom come.

And those people from all over the world said, "We want in! Tell us what to do!"

So Peter answered:

> "Change your life. Turn to God and be baptized, each of you, in the name of Jesus Christ, so your sins are forgiven. Receive the gift of the Holy Spirit. The promise is targeted to you and your children, but also to all who are far away—whomever, in fact, our Master God invites."[4]

The Bible says, "That day about three thousand took him at his word, were baptized and were signed up. They committed themselves to the teaching of the apostles, the life together, the common meal, and the prayers."[5] They became the First Church of Jerusalem—and the First Church of Mesopotamia, First Church of Judea, the First Church of Cappadocia, the First Church of Pontus and Asia, the First Church of Phrygia and Pamphylia, and the First Church of Egypt and Libya and Rome.

That day, they became part of something much bigger than themselves. Unimaginably bigger. Infinitely bigger. They became "the city of the living God, the heavenly Jerusalem."[6] They united with "countless thousands of angels in a joyful gathering."[7] They joined "the assembly of God's firstborn children, whose names are written in heaven."[8] They inherited "a kingdom that is unshakable,"[9] "a kingdom that will never be destroyed."[10]

Everyone who experiences new life through faith in Jesus Christ inherits the kingdom. If that describes you, then you are a part of something bigger than yourself—the church. That means that all those things described in the previous paragraph are true of you. They are not things you can deserve; they are not things you can earn. But they *are* things you can live out. They are things of which you can become more aware. They are things you can more fully appreciate and more purposefully put into practice by more fully participating in the life of your church.

Church Can Help You Find a Place of Meaningful Service

As mentioned in chapter three, every follower of Jesus has a unique mix of talents, skills, and gifts. Those abilities, together with your background, experiences, and personality, have equipped you to fill a crucial place and perform a meaningful function in your church, community, and world.

You may have planned to play major league baseball when you were running the bases on the sandlot or on your high school baseball diamond, but God may have known all along that you would make a great coach for inner-city kids. You may have thought you'd never again use your training as a dental assistant once you had kids and decided to homeschool...until you learned that your church's short-term mission trips to Peru included free dental clinics for the poor in the pueblos. You may have been unable to see any purpose or plan in your history of abusive relationships, until you discovered how rewarding it is to comfort and counsel those who are suffering in ways you know only too well.

The Bible says,

> There are different kinds of working, but in all of them and in everyone it is the same God at work.

Now to each one the manifestation of the Spirit is given for the common good. To one there is given through the Spirit a message of wisdom, to another a message of knowledge by means of the same Spirit, to another faith by the same Spirit, to another gifts of healing by that one Spirit, to another miraculous powers, to another prophecy, to another distinguishing between spirits, to another speaking in different kinds of tongues and to still another the interpretation of tongues. All these are the work of one and the same Spirit, and he distributes them to each one, just as he determines.[11]

But here's the thing: God intends for those gifts and abilities to be used and amplified in and through the church, just as He intends for your arm or leg to work as part of a larger unit:

> The human body has many parts, but the many parts make up one whole body. So it is with the body of Christ.... The body has many different parts, not just one part. If the foot says, "I am not a part of the body because I am not a hand," that does not make it any less a part of the body. And if the ear says, "I am not part of the body because I am not an eye," would that make it any less a part of the body? If the whole body were an eye, how would you hear? Or if your whole body were an ear, how would you smell anything?
>
> But our bodies have many parts, and God has put each part just where he wants it. How strange a body would be if it had only one part! Yes, there are many parts, but only one body. The eye can never say to the hand, "I don't need you." The head can't say to the feet, "I don't need you."[12]

You need the church and the church needs you. The church will help you find a place—or places—of meaningful service. You will help the church function better as a whole. In God's wise plan, you and those around you will be better off if you find a place of meaningful service. It can change you. It can change your church. It can change your community. It can even change the world.

Henrietta Mears had wanted to be a missionary. She had trained to be a high school chemistry teacher. However, it was when she started teaching a Sunday school class that she found the ideal intersection of her skills, talents, training, gifts, personality, and passion. Soon after she started teaching on Sundays, attendance began to swell, and in a few years it reached four thousand. Over the years, she influenced more than four hundred young people who entered full-time Christian service. One of them was Bill Bright, the founder of Campus Crusade for Christ.

Unhappy with the available lessons, Henrietta and her helpers began writing their own materials. Soon, requests for copies began flowing in. Her office staff couldn't keep up with the demand, so she and a group of businessmen started Gospel Light Publications, one of the first publishers of Christian education materials.

When she felt the need for a Christian retreat center Henrietta prayed and dreamed big, eventually establishing Forest Home. It was there that a young preacher named Billy Graham resolved his doubts about the Bible before launching his Los Angeles evangelistic crusade in 1949. Graham would later say that no woman except his mother and wife had a greater impact on his life.

And it all began with a woman finding a meaningful place of service in her church's Sunday school. As she would later say, "God doesn't call us to sit on the sidelines and watch. He calls us to be on the field, playing the games."[13]

Church Can Help You Pool and Magnify Your Giving for Maximum Impact

In the earliest days of the church's existence, something amazing happened that should be a powerful and continual example for us. The first historian of the church said,

And all the believers lived in a wonderful harmony, holding everything in common. They sold whatever they owned and pooled their resources so that each person's need was met.[14]

That writer (whose name was Luke) says virtually the same thing just two chapters later:

The whole congregation of believers was united as one—one heart, one mind! They didn't even claim ownership of their own possessions. No one said, "That's mine; you can't have it." They shared everything. The apostles gave powerful witness to the resurrection of the Master Jesus, and grace was on all of them.

And so it turned out that not a person among them was needy. Those who owned fields or houses sold them and brought the price of the sale to the apostles and made an offering of it. The apostles then distributed it according to each person's need.[15]

Interesting, isn't it, that Luke would point out this phenomenon *twice*? It is even more remarkable when you consider that Luke (who also penned the gospel—the life story of Jesus—that bears his name) was a careful historian; it is highly unlikely that he twice mentioned the early church's pooling of resources unintentionally or absent-mindedly.

It's almost as if he was leading somewhere.

He was. Two chapters later, in Acts 6, Luke tells the story of the selection of the first church deacons, or business managers. The circumstances that led to these new positions being created are described in Acts 6:1–7:

But as the believers rapidly multiplied, there were rumblings of discontent. The Greek-speaking believers complained about the Hebrew-speaking believers, saying that their widows were being discriminated against in the daily distribution of food.

So the Twelve called a meeting of all the believers. They said, "We apostles should spend our time teaching the word of God, not running a food program. And so, brothers, select seven men who are well respected and are full of the Spirit and wisdom. We will give them this responsibility. Then we apostles can spend our time in prayer and teaching the word."

Everyone liked this idea, and they chose the following: Stephen (a man full of faith and the Holy Spirit), Philip, Procorus, Nicanor, Timon, Parmenas, and Nicolas of Antioch (an earlier convert to the Jewish faith). These seven were presented to the apostles, who prayed for them as they laid their hands on them.

So God's message continued to spread. The number of believers greatly increased in Jerusalem, and many of the Jewish priests were converted, too.[16]

Those verses depict the very practical impact of those first Christians' generosity and cooperation: The widows among them—both Jewish and non-Jewish, racially speaking—were cared for on a daily basis. (In those days, there were no pensions, Social Security, Medicare, or other "safety nets"; when a woman lost her husband, the extended family had to provide for her—but if she became a Christian, her family would disown her, leaving her destitute.)

So Luke's frequent mention of those early Christians giving selflessly and pooling their resources was intentional. It revealed how God worked in them to achieve maximum impact. In fact, the impact was so great that three hundred years later, the most powerful man on earth, the Roman Emperor Julian, noted that the church's influence had grown. Referring to the followers of Jesus as "Galileans," he wrote,

> It is a disgrace to us that no Jew has to beg, and that every Galilean is ready to provide support for our poor as well as their own, while men laugh that we cannot

muster aid for our people.[17]

Don't miss the fact that Julian was the emperor of *Rome*. And yet he lamented that the followers of Jesus cared not only for their own poor, but also for those the emperor called "our poor." How could those Christians—in the minority and often persecuted—embarrass the rich mighty Roman empire by taking better care of the poor than they did?

The answer is in the text. They pooled their resources, and thus had a far greater impact on the world than any individual follower of Jesus could have done. And that has been the case throughout history. Churches have started clinics and hospitals, rehabilitation centers and feeding programs, colleges and universities, and missions and missionaries—Operation Carelift, Samaritan's Purse, The Salvation Army, World Vision, Compassion International, The Water Project, and many more. The list could go on for pages, and is amplified by the efforts of thousands of churches that are giving and going all over the world to cure and prevent disease, ease hunger, adopt children, clothe the poor, stop human trafficking, transform economies, change lives, and change the world.

Church offers you an opportunity to amplify the impact of your giving and expand the reach of your influence. By participating in and cooperating with your church, you can amaze yourself—and perhaps even shame emperors!—by joining your interests, passions, efforts, and resources with others, for maximum impact.

In fact, why not get started now? Chances are, your church sponsors a missionary in some distant land. Why not find out who that is and what they need? Your church may be close to the scene of a recent disaster; why not enlist others to send money or supplies through the Salvation Army? The possibilities are almost endless, and though the resources may seem meager at first, remember that the head of the church is the One who multiplied a few loaves and fishes into a meal for thousands. He can do the same with your offering when it is placed in His hands.

Church Can Help You Discern and Enlist in What God Is Doing in the World

One of the most exciting things involvement in a church can do for you is to help you discern—and enlist in what God is doing in the world today. It is so easy, in the course of our hectic and insulated daily lives, to forget that God is always at work. Once, when Jesus' fiercest enemies harassed Him for healing a man on the Sabbath, Jesus said, "My Father is always working, and I too must work."[18]

Imagine what it would have been like to hand the nail to Martin Luther when he hammered his Ninety-Five Theses to the church door in Wittenberg, Germany, unleashing a wildfire of reformation throughout the Western world.

Imagine having been in the meeting when a young English shoemaker named William Carey proposed an effort to reach people around the world who had never heard the good news of Jesus Christ and was told, "Young man, sit down! When God pleases to convert the heathen, he'll do it without consulting you or me." Or envision sponsoring the printing of his response, *An Enquiry into the Obligations of Christians to Use Means for the Conversion of the Heathens,* which laid the theological foundation of modern missions. Picture accompanying him to India, where he translated and printed the Scriptures in forty-four native languages and dialects, helped end the practices of infant sacrifice and widow burning, established numerous churches and mission stations, started the influential Serampore College, formed a hundred rural schools (which also encouraged the education of girls), printed the first Indian newspaper, and inspired a new era of similar missionary efforts worldwide.

Imagine being able to support the efforts of William Wilberforce, who was instrumental in abolishing slavery throughout the British Empire. Visualize helping Harriet Tubman, the former slave who made twenty or more rescue missions into American slave states to lead more than three hundred men, women, and children to freedom. Or think about proofreading the early drafts of *Uncle Tom's Cabin,* the book by a preacher's daughter that pierced a nation's complacency and exposed many to the evils of slavery.

Imagine enlisting in a young William Booth's efforts to evangelize and care for London's thieves, prostitutes, gamblers, and drunkards, which gave rise to The Salvation Army. Perhaps volunteering in Billy Graham's inaugural mass evangelism crusade in 1949. Or showing up on the Asbury College campus one morning in 1970 when a routine student chapel service turned into a prayer meeting that lasted for weeks and spread across the United States and into foreign countries.

Imagine being a part of what God plans to do next, perhaps in your community, or in Africa, Asia, and Latin America, from which it is estimated 90 percent of the next generation of Christ-followers will come. On your own, of course, you might stumble into such an exhilarating opportunity, but as a part of the church, you are much more likely to hear the news, feel the winds of change, and join the effort—big or small, local or global—in whatever God does next.

"AND ONE WAS THERE WHO THE ROADS DID KNOW, AND THAT ONE SHOWED HIM THE WAY TO GO."
—SADIE TILLER CRAWLEY

CHAPTER 8

PREPARE

Thor Heyerdahl was an ethnographer and adventurer who wanted to demonstrate that ancient people could have made sea voyages across great distances in relatively primitive vessels, linking otherwise distant and separate cultures.

In 1947, Heyerdahl and five friends set out from Peru on a wooden raft made from native materials that would have been available to ancient South Americans.

They called it the Kon-Tiki, which they planned to sail five thousand miles across the Pacific Ocean.

Once the raft was built, the crew assembled supplies and provisions for the journey that would take more than three months, according to their calculations. Heyerdahl described their preparations:

> A few days before we sailed, provisions and water and all our equipment were stowed on board the raft. We took provisions for six men for four months, in the form of solid little cardboard cartons containing military rations. Herman had the idea of boiling asphalt and pouring it so as to make a level layer round each separate carton. Then we strewed sand on the cartons, to prevent them from sticking together, and stowed them, packed close, under the bamboo deck where they filled the space between the nine low crossbeams which supported the deck.
>
> At a crystal-clear spring high up in the mountains, we filled fifty-six small water cans with 275 gallons of drinking water. These, too, we made fast in between the crossbeams so that the sea might always splash around them. On the bamboo deck we lashed fast the

rest of the equipment including large wicker baskets full of fruit, roots, and coconuts.

Knut and Torstein took one corner of the bamboo cabin for the radio, and inside the hut, down between the crossbeams, we made fast eight boxes. Two were reserved for scientific instruments and films; the other six were allotted one to each of us, with an intimation that each man could take with him as much private property as he could find room for in his own box. As Erik had brought several rolls of drawing paper and a guitar, his box was so full that he had to put his stockings in Torstein's. It took four seamen to carry Bengt's on board. He brought nothing but books but he had managed to cram in seventy-three sociological and ethnological works. We laid plaited reed mats and our straw mattresses on top of the boxes and then we were ready to start.

All that preparation. All those provisions. So much thought and consideration, and yet, even with their careful planning, Heyerdahl later admitted that he repeatedly feared for his life on the 101-day, 4,340-mile journey, which eventually ended on an uninhabited island in the Tuamotu Archipelago of French Polynesia.

It was an epic adventure that has since been celebrated in literature, song, and film. And, though it proved Heyerdahl's theory was possible, it didn't persuade the scientific and historical community who believe today that the ethnology of the Pacific Islands is rooted in Asia rather than South America.

But nonetheless, Heyerdahl's success began with long and careful preparation. If it hadn't, it is unlikely the crew—who all safely reached their destination—would have survived. In fact, without all those preparations, it is unlikely we would have ever heard of them.

And yet, many of us face life's journey with minimal preparation. We may be turning a corner or heading into a new season in life. We've started a new relationship or are contemplating a career shift. The kids are growing up. We'll soon face an empty nest. The economy is changing. Our parents are aging.

Our priorities are changing. Our vistas are expanding. If we're like most people, we have been so wrapped up in just keeping up with the other cars on the road that we have given little thought to the twists and turns that lie ahead.

The question isn't even, "Are there dangers and opportunities on the road ahead?" We may take it for granted that there are both. The question is, "Do I have the resources to meet them?" That is where the church can make a huge difference in your life.

Church Can Lay the Foundation for Your Future

Alex is a pastor's kid. Like many PKs, he often struggled with the expectations and pressures of trying to conform to people's expectations of him. He kept attending church through his teen years, because his parents required him to, but vowed to do his own thing when he went off to college, and he did. He attended school far away from home and church and never once attended any of the churches in his college town. Yet a funny thing happened. The people who kept in touch with him during his college years weren't friends from his old school or neighborhood, but people from his church back home. They called and e-mailed. They sent care packages. Several even traveled a long way to visit him. When he graduated and moved back to his hometown, folks from church helped him find a job. They introduced him to a young woman who had joined the church while he was away, who later became his wife. They enlisted him into the worship ministry at church, which renewed a long-dormant relationship with God and ignited a new passion and purpose in his life. And when his father was no longer pastor and the worship leader position came open, guess who applied and got the job?

Alex never suspected that his involvement in the church was laying the foundation for his future. He never would have guessed that those years as a reluctant churchgoer were preparing him for a future as an enthusiastic church staff member. And he could not have imagined that the church he thought he had left behind would introduce him to the woman of his dreams.

Not everyone meets his or her future spouse at church, of course. Not everyone ends up on staff at a church.

But wherever you are in your life's journey, church involvement can lay the foundation for your future, one way or another. It may be by learning from others who've been where you are—or where you hope to go.

Debbie says she came to the church as a "messed-up teenager." It was in the church, she says, "that I learned what love is from the pastors and many faithful members who soon became my brothers and sisters and spiritual grandmas. These people showed me hope. They nurtured my self-esteem and helped me believe that I could be different and better. With their encouragement, I became a youth leader in my church and learned to love others the way I had been loved. With their support, I entered ministry. And despite years of abuse and dysfunctional family systems, they modeled and taught me how to build a strong marriage and become a good parent."

Churches still do those sorts of things today. Every day. Whatever passage lies ahead of you, there are people in the church who have traveled that way before and have wisdom and counsel to offer you. Whatever preparations are called for in getting you out of where you are or getting you where you want to go, the church is a rich resource for helping you to wisely pack your raft.

Church Can Be a Comfort and Resource at Life's Crossroads

Her name was Bonnie. Her husband and sons were involved in a local church, but she and her daughter held back. The pastor approached Bonnie about the activities of the church's youth group and how he hoped her daughter might join in on some of the things that were planned. But Bonnie smiled and shook her head and said, "My daughter is a lot like me. She doesn't need other people in her life."

The pastor was momentarily flummoxed and Bonnie walked on. He wanted to call after her. He wanted to chase her down and tell her she was not only cheating herself, but also her daughter. Even pastors don't always have a quick and ready answer.

"I should have followed up with her," he says now. "Even though I look back and see that it wouldn't have done any good, I still wish I had given her a chance to see the danger she was in. And the danger she was putting her daughter in."

Unfortunately, however, he didn't. A couple of years after that short conversation, Bonnie faced a crisis that tore apart her marriage and devastated her family, especially her daughter, the youngest of her children. When that happened, she and her daughter suffered deeply—and largely alone—because they had no network of support. Their extended family lived hundreds of miles away. They had no close friendships. They had no one to turn to. No family of faith to comfort and care for them through their ordeal. Though some from the church tried, they were rudely rebuffed.

How different it could have been. Whether or not Bonnie's crisis could have been averted, at that crucial crossroad in her life—and her daughter's life—she could have received comfort and counsel, help and hope from a loving supportive church family.

The pastor and poet John Donne wrote,

> No man is an island, entire of itself;
> every man is a piece of the continent,
> a part of the main.
> If a clod be washed away by the sea, Europe is the less,
> as well as if a promontory were,
> as well as if a manor of thy friend's
> or of thine own were.
> Any man's death diminishes me,
> because I am involved in mankind;
> and therefore never send to know for whom
> the bell tolls;
> it tolls for thee.[1]

When you come to a crossroad in your life, the church can be both a comfort and resource. Brenda and her husband had been married seventeen years, and though neither had regularly attended church in that time, Brenda would occasionally accompany Sandy, a friend from work, to a Sunday morning service. She never joined Sandy's church, but she got to know the pastors and would sometimes recognize people from the church at Starbucks or in a local restaurant.

So when Brenda's sixteen-year-old son died in an early morning auto accident on the way to school, she told the funeral director to call the pastor of Sandy's church. Brenda didn't know how these things worked; she had no Plan B if the pastor couldn't perform the ceremony, but the pastor and his wife did more than that. They supported the family during the long hours of visitation. The church mobilized to provide a meal after the funeral for visiting family and friends from out of town. They arranged for meals to be dropped off daily to Brenda's house for the next week. Sandy coordinated periodic "check-ins" by various church members, who stopped by, called, and sent cards in the months after the funeral.

"On the day of the funeral, we didn't really know anyone in the church besides Sandy," Brenda says, "but I don't know how we could have survived without them. We had friends, and family, too, but that church knew how to support us in ways our other friends and family didn't."

Five months after her son's accident, Brenda persuaded her husband to attend an Easter service with her, the first time they'd ever attended a Sunday worship service together. They weren't sure what to expect. As they entered the church, they met so many people who had supported them through the funeral and the grieving process, it felt like a reunion—and it was. Before long, Brenda became a follower of Jesus, and today is part of the team that takes meals to new parents and grieving families.

Churches advertise all sorts of things: Christmas plays, sermons, church sales, and so on. However, maybe what they ought to advertise is this: "We'll be here for you." For a funeral. Your child's wedding. When you wonder whether to move Mom in with you or find her a good nursing facility. When you open your new business. When you close your business. When you're hoping to adopt a child. When you're facing retirement. When you are at a crossroad, the church can be an indispensable comfort and resource.

Church Can Prepare You for the Unexpected

The Bible says, "You do not know what your life will be like tomorrow."[2] Or, as Kenny Loggins sings, "No one can tell what the future holds."[3] We may well say, "Ain't that the truth?"

Think about it: What were you doing on November 8, 1989? Do you remember? That was the day before the Berlin Wall fell. Did you expect it? Could you have guessed? Did it grab your attention? Affect your plans?

What about the day before the 9/11 terrorist attacks in the United States? Do you remember where you were? What you were planning? Did you have travel plans? Did you have any inkling of what the next twenty-four hours would hold for you? for the United States and the world?

Or how about Christmas Day, 2004? Did you have any notion of how many lives would change the next day, when a catastrophic earthquake and tsunami devastated many areas in Southeast Asia, including Indonesia, Sri Lanka, India, Thailand, the Maldives, and more?

How about June 28, 2007? That was the day before Apple released the first iPhone and introduced a new era of technology.

Perhaps March 10, 2011 rings a bell, the day before an 8.9 magnitude earthquake struck Japan and spawned a tsunami, which in turn caused a nuclear disaster at the Fukushima Dai-ichi nuclear power station?

What about May 19, 2013, a quiet spring Sunday? That was the day before an EF5 tornado with wind speeds over two hundred miles per hour hit Moore, Oklahoma, carving a seventeen-mile path of destruction, leaving a community stunned and grieving.

Did you know those things were coming? Did you have an idea of how much the world—perhaps *your* world, even—was about to change? Was there anyone or anything there to help you prepare for the unexpected?

One way to read the history of the early church (in the Bible book called Acts) is as a catalog of the unexpected. When the first followers of Jesus gathered in the Upper Room after His ascension into heaven, they knew to expect something—but whatever they expected, it wasn't what happened (Acts 1–2).

When those first church folk started pooling their resources and eliminating destitution and poverty among them, they didn't expect what happened next (Acts 5).

When the church selected the first deacons, or business managers, to make sure the Greek-speaking widows were taken care of, they didn't expect one of those deacons to become the first martyr in church history (Acts 6–7).

When persecution hit the church, they surely didn't expect the authorities' main "enforcer" to become a follower of Jesus (Acts 9).

When Peter moved to Joppa, he couldn't have imagined that he would be in the ideal location to facilitate the Gentile Pentecost, the sending of God's Holy Spirit on non-Jews living in the Roman resort town of Caesarea (Acts 10).

When Peter was arrested and thrown into prison, he probably would have been surprised if someone had told him that King Herod would be dead before Peter! But that is what happened (Acts 11).

And on it goes. None of us knows what tomorrow holds. We do not know what our lives will be like twenty-four hours from now. The unexpected awaits. But, while we cannot know the future, we can know—and consult—the One who does know. The psalmist David wrote,

> Before a word is on my tongue
> you, LORD, know it completely.
> You hem me in behind and before,
> and you lay your hand upon me.
> Such knowledge is too wonderful for me,
> too lofty for me to attain.[4]

When the church gathers to worship and work, to sing and study, God is there. Not only that, but He is "behind and before." He is leading the way and bringing up the rear. That doesn't mean that He will always tell the church what is about to happen, but sometimes He will.

After the events mentioned above from the book of Acts, it then records this:

The congregation in Antioch was blessed with a number of prophet-preachers and teachers:

Barnabas,
Simon, nicknamed Niger,
Lucius the Cyrenian,
Manaen, an advisor to the ruler Herod,
Saul.

One day as they were worshiping God—they were also fasting as they waited for guidance—the Holy Spirit spoke: "Take Barnabas and Saul and commission them for the work I have called them to do."

So they commissioned them. In that circle of intensity and obedience, of fasting and praying, they laid hands on their heads and sent them off.[5]

Barnabas and Saul (later called Paul) may not have expected that. They may have made plans to open a store together, or something else. But God spoke. And He did it to and through the church. He apparently didn't tell Barnabas. There is no indication that God gave Saul a heads-up. He spoke through the gathered church and the unexpected suddenly became history.

There is something else at work in that passage. A few chapters before, the author of Acts records how Saul—who had been the main enforcer of persecution against the church until he encountered the risen Jesus Christ (Acts 9) and became a follower of Jesus himself—experienced some distrust from the church when he came back to Jerusalem and tried to join it. That is understandable, of course. No one wants to be framed or arrested or tortured. Who would have wanted to take the chance that "Saul the Enforcer" was undercover, and just pretending to be a follower of Jesus?

However, Acts says this: "Barnabas took him under his wing."[6]

In other words, Barnabas accepted him and became a sort of

sponsor. He introduced him around. He encouraged him. He prepared him. So when—sometime later—God's Holy Spirit announced that Barnabas and Saul were to be sent off as missionaries, Saul was prepared for the unexpected turn of events.

God had been working the whole time, of course. He is never taken off guard. The unexpected is never a surprise to Him. Though Saul may have been clueless—and probably even Barnabas—God was patiently and purposefully working in and through the church to prepare Saul for the next turn in the road.

God can do the same with you—*for* you. "You do not know what your life will be like tomorrow,"[7] but God does. He may have just the right person—or people—in position to prepare you for whatever comes next. He may have the whole church in a position to take you under their wing, so to speak. Or He may intend for you to take someone under your wing, and prepare both of you for some unexpected development.

Who knows? Not you, that's for sure.

But God is working.

The unexpected is coming.

And the church may just be the means God uses to speak to you, to prepare you, and to meet, embrace, and conquer the unexpected.

"TAKE REST; A FIELD THAT HAS RESTED GIVES A BOUNTIFUL CROP."
—OVID

CHAPTER 9

RECOVER

It is woven into the fabric of Creation. Built into the nature of things. Though many of us are still learning to recognize and obey it.

Music—whether a sprightly birdsong, a rap lyric, or a majestic symphony—does not consist only of the notes that are struck. The beauty occurs in the artful interplay between sounds and non-sounds. Rests are as important in the creation of music as notes. The drummer must lift his stick or mallet. The trumpeter must inhale in order to exhale. The vocalist must punctuate her notes with "silences on either side,"[1] or her music becomes noise.

Farmers understand this principle, too. A field that is planted every year without a rest will yield less and less as the years go by. Wise farmers allow part of their land to remain unplanted during a growing season, so the soil can recover its vitality, restoring its moisture and mineral content so that a better crop will be produced in the years that follow.

Experienced athletes know that their bodies cannot train and exercise constantly. They know that they cannot achieve the highest levels of performance unless they allow—or even force—themselves to take a day off from exercise on a regular basis. The human body is not constructed for constant stress and activity; recovery times allow the body to replenish its energy stores, repair tissues that have broken down, and restore fluids that have been depleted during times of physical exertion. The respite between workouts is as key to training and improving as the workouts themselves.

The human brain's ability to focus and concentrate is also dependent on regular—even strategic—recovery periods. Particularly for denizens of the twenty-first century who live such hectic lives with constant noise and stimuli and distraction and disruption that the brain can become over-whelmed, overloaded, forgetful, and flighty. A recent study further confirms what scientists have long suggested: brain functions can be restored and renewed by specific recovery techniques such as a stroll through a park. Dr. Jenny Roe, a professor who oversaw the study, says that "going for a walk in a green space or just sitting, or even viewing green spaces from your office window...is likely to have a restorative effect and help with attention fatigue and stress recovery."[2]

What is true of music and soil, of the body and brain, is also true of life. From time to time, we all feel depleted, even beat up. We may need time and space to lick our wounds. We need more than a day off or a vacation from work; we need recovery. We may require resources outside ourselves to recover from things like addiction, depression, or divorce. Even if we're riding high right now, we know we can't keep going like this indefinitely, without a break, without reprieve...without finding a way to recover some of the things we've lost.

Church Can Be a Place to Reclaim "Paradise Lost"

The first pages of the Bible depict the earliest chapters of human history, when the first man and woman lived in a peaceful, luxuriant paradise, free from want, fear, stress, and sadness. Their days were filled with discovery and beauty. They enjoyed perfect intimacy with each other and with God.

The Bible doesn't tell us how long those idyllic days lasted. Maybe they went on for months. Maybe years, or longer. Eventually, though, evil intruded. Temptation appeared to those first humans. They succumbed. They sinned. As a result of their sin, they lost their innocence. They lost their joy. They lost perfection. They lost paradise.[3]

The loss has been felt ever since. We all feel it. We know in our bones that this world—*as it is*—is not as it should be. We know there is something wrong, dreadfully wrong, all around us. We know that war and hatred are a part of what is wrong with things. So are bigotry and racism, poverty and disease.

We know, too, that not only is something wrong in the world, there is something wrong in each of us. There is no paradise inside us. There are doubts and fears, hurts and hatreds, pride and lust, among other bad things. Things that are hurtful to others and unhealthy to us.

However, the Bible does not leave us there. It not only tells the story of paradise lost; it reveals paradise regained. In fact, just as the first chapters of the Bible explain the loss of paradise on earth, the final chapters describe the restoration of paradise for the whole earth.[4] And virtually all of the chapters in between portray God's hopes and dreams for you, and your own personal "paradise regained." They speak of peace with God. They speak of hope, glory, and overwhelming love.[5] They tell how:

> When we were utterly helpless, Christ came at just the right time and died for us sinners. Now, most people would not be willing to die for an upright person, though someone might perhaps be willing to die for a person who is especially good. But God showed his great love for us by sending Christ to die for us while we were still sinners…. So now we can rejoice in our wonderful new relationship with God because our Lord Jesus Christ has made us friends of God.
>
> When Adam sinned, sin entered the world. Adam's sin brought death, so death spread to everyone, for everyone sinned…. Now Adam is a symbol, a representation of Christ, who was yet to come. But there is a great difference between Adam's sin and God's gracious gift. For the sin of this one man, Adam, brought death to many. But even greater is God's wonderful grace and his gift of forgiveness to many through this other man, Jesus Christ. And the result of God's gracious gift is very different from the result of that one man's sin. For Adam's sin led to condemnation, but God's free gift leads to our being made right with God, even though we are guilty of many sins. For the sin of this one man, Adam, caused death to rule over many. But even greater is God's wonderful grace and his gift of righteousness,

for all who receive it will live in triumph over sin and death through this one man, Jesus Christ. Yes, Adam's one sin brings condemnation for everyone, but Christ's one act of righteousness brings a right relationship with God and new life for everyone.[6]

As a result of God's grace, fulfilled in Jesus Christ's obedience and sacrifice, paradise can come again to your heart and life. Relationship with God can be restored, and new peace, hope, glory, and overwhelming love fill your spirit and life. If you haven't yet experienced that good news, that return to paradise in your heart, the church can help you regain what was lost. In fact, it can begin this moment, if you sincerely call out to God, saying, "Lord Jesus, I need You. Thank You for dying on the cross for my sins. I open the door of my life and receive You as my Savior and Lord. Thank You for forgiving my sins and giving me eternal life. Take control of my life from this moment on, and make me the kind of person You want me to be."

There is nothing magical about that prayer. It isn't an incantation. But if it reflects the desire and intention of your heart, then you may trust God to fulfill all the beauty and power of Romans 5 (the Bible passage quoted above) in your life. But it doesn't stop there because the church exists to help you learn to enjoy all the blessings, privileges, and responsibilities that are included in your new life. Therefore, it is important that you tell someone in your church—the church that gave you this book, perhaps—about your commitment and enlist their help in letting peace, hope, glory, and overwhelming love rule your heart and life. Then, the words of John Milton, the English poet who wrote the classics, *Paradise Lost* and *Paradise Regained*, will be true for you:

> I WHO erewhile the happy garden sung,
> By one man's disobedience lost, now sing
> Recovered Paradise to all mankind,
> By one man's firm obedience fully tried
> Through all temptation, and the Tempter foiled
> In all his wiles, defeated and repulsed,
> And Eden raised in the waste wilderness.[7]

Church Can Be a Place to Recoup and Rest from Life's Stresses

The ninth chapter of Acts in the Bible contains the first of several accounts of Saul—the great persecutor who tried to wipe out the early church with fear and violence—traveling to Damascus (a journey of about 135 miles from Jerusalem) to arrest any followers of Jesus there and "bring them back to Jerusalem in chains."[8]

On his way there, however, a brilliant light appeared in the sky and Saul fell off his horse. He heard a voice calling his name and asking, "Why are you persecuting me?" The speaker identified himself as "Jesus, the one you are persecuting,"[9] and told Saul to continue to Damascus and await further instructions.

Moments later, when Saul stood up, he discovered he was blind. He needed help from others in his entourage to finish his journey. Once he arrived in Damascus, he stayed with a man named Judas, hoping for his sight to return. He fasted. He prayed.

Finally, as he prayed, he saw a vision of a man named Ananias, a follower of Jesus—one of those Saul had come to Damascus to arrest. In the vision, Ananias laid his hands on Saul's head and prayed for his sight to be restored.

Saul had been blind for three days when that vision became a reality. A man came to him, identified himself, and laid his hands on Saul's head. "Brother Saul," he said, "the Lord Jesus, who appeared to you on the road, has sent me so that you might regain your sight and be filled with the Holy Spirit."[10]

At that, the Bible says, "something like scales" instantly dropped from Saul's eyes, and he could see again. He wasted no time in being baptized. And then, the Bible says, "He ate some food and regained his strength."[11]

Saul had been through a stressful period. He had encountered the risen, exalted Jesus, which must have been simultaneously amazing and frightening. He had been knocked down a peg or two—literally. He had suffered a loss. And to top it all off, his job security was in serious doubt.

It is interesting, though, that Jesus told Saul to finish his journey; He could have turned him around and sent him back to Jerusalem. It is interesting that He told him to await further instructions in Damascus; He could have explained everything to Saul right there on the road. It is interesting that He made Saul wait three days for the visit from Ananias; He could have sent help on day one. It is interesting that Jesus brought about Saul's healing—and baptism, and perhaps even his first meal in three days—through Ananias; Jesus could have done it all Himself, at any moment.

We can't know for sure why Jesus did things that way. The way He worked seems to illustrate how the church can often be a source of rest and recuperation. While Saul received a vision from God, he received his sight only through Ananias, a member of the church Saul was persecuting. While Saul prayed throughout his stay at Judas' house, he received the Holy Spirit when Ananias prayed for him. He received baptism through Ananias. He "regained his strength" after he came into contact with the church, in the person of Ananias, and "stayed with the believers in Damascus for a few days."[12]

As it was for Saul, so it can be for you. The church can be a place of rest for you. It can be a place to encourage recuperation from the stress and strife of your world.

Kasey Hitt, a spiritual director and retreat leader in Nashville, Tennessee, has witnessed firsthand the difference a church can make for people who need rest and recuperation.

> "I've seen the church beautifully fulfill its role as a place of respite, restoration, and healing by giving people (including the leaders of the church themselves) permission to rest (which is to say trust), by extending a pastoral invitation to pursue rest through the week, and by offering tools to help people 'be still and know.'[13] I've seen the church do this through silent retreats, spiritual direction, spaces of silence in worship, and classes on prayer, discernment, and even breathing techniques. I've seen church council meetings begin with times of meditation to transition from the noisy world so that leaders can rest and listen.

"Some people won't consider going to church or becoming involved in a church because they assume it is just going to add to the overstimulation of their already noisy, busy lives. And, of course, sometimes that is the case. But as a spiritual director who has a particular calling to pastors, church staffs, and church leaders, I've seen the indescribable blessing that results when leaders and churches become places and people of rest and restoration. This is what each of us is called to be, as followers of the one who said, 'Come to me...and I will give you rest.'[14] Especially in this day and age, in this world, we all need places where we can let our guards down, rest our weary souls, and breathe again."[15]

How do you know if a church can be that place for you? Kasey suggests that this takes discernment. "Ask yourself, after visiting a church for a season, 'Do I sense permission to put down my smart phone? To let down my guard? To be myself? And do I show myself to be a safe place, a refuge, to others? Can I contribute somehow to making this church a place of rest, a place to recuperate? And if so, how?'"

Church Can Be a Place of Renewal, Revival, and Resurrection

Every church has at least one. Every small town does, too. A person everyone just loves. A person who is always there, always helping, always smiling and encouraging others. In the coastal town of Joppa, that person's name was Tabitha.

Her name meant "gazelle," an apt description of her character and grace. When someone was sick, she would show up with a pot of lentil soup. When a friend needed encouragement, she would make her a new dress or coat. When a tear fell, she was ready with a hug. When someone died, she stayed with the family day and night. When a need arose, she was there, which meant she was well known and much loved among the poor in town.

But one day illness struck her, and before anyone knew how serious it was, she died. No one could believe it. The church—the whole town, it seemed—was in shock. Her friends prepared her body for burial and laid her in an upstairs room.

Two men in the Joppa church, knowing that Peter was staying in the neighboring town of Lydda, went there to find him. They begged him to stop whatever he was doing and come as quickly as he could.

When Peter arrived at Tabitha's house with the men, they led him upstairs, where grieving women encircled the room. They swarmed Peter, crying and begging him to help. Each one was wearing something Tabitha had made as a gift; one after another showed him the tokens of her kindness.

Peter listened patiently and then asked them all to leave the room. He knelt at the window and prayed. Then he stood and turned to face the body. "Arise, Tabitha," he said. She opened her eyes, blinked, focused on Peter, and then she sat up and swung her legs over the side of the bier. He extended his hand and she stood. He smiled and called to the others to come back in the room.[16]

That incident, described in the ninth chapter of Acts, parallels another facet of the church. It can be a place of new life for you. It can revive you and restore you.

Everyone's energy flags from time to time. Everyone's vitality ebbs and flows. The causes and sources of those comings and goings are often as mysterious as the ocean's tides. But regular involvement in a church will make times of renewal and revival more frequent, if not necessarily more predictable.

Maybe it's happened to you. The power goes out. Everything shuts off. But you were planning to leave anyway, so you leave the house. When you come back later, the lights are on, the digital clocks are flashing, and power is flowing again. You wonder how long the power was off and when it was restored, but you don't know, of course, because you weren't there when it happened.

Renewal and revival is something like that. If you are involved in the church and don't give up when times of spiritual powerlessness hit you, you will be present when the power returns. If you stay in the "upper room" when dryness or dead-ness seems to overtake you, you will be ready when the time comes to "arise."

Everyone needs that from time to time; however, many people miss out because they go "A.W.O.L." when the lights go out and the power seems to stop flowing. Those who hang in there, though, will sooner or later experience the renewal, revival—and even resurrection—that God sends to His faithful, worshiping, praying, waiting children.

Church Can Be a Place to Recover from Addictions, Abuse, and More

The same passage in the Bible that tells of Tabitha's restoration to life relates the story of a man named Aeneas:

> Peter went off on a mission to visit all the churches. In the course of his travels he arrived in Lydda and met with the believers there. He came across a man—his name was Aeneas—who had been in bed eight years paralyzed. Peter said, "Aeneas, Jesus Christ heals you. Get up and make your bed!" And he did it—jumped right out of bed. Everybody who lived in Lydda and Sharon saw him walking around and woke up to the fact that God was alive and active among them.[17]

Can you imagine? Paralyzed for eight years. Bedridden day after day. For almost three thousand days. The Bible doesn't say what caused his paralysis. Was it a workplace accident? a stroke? a tumor? We don't know. But whatever the cause, the man experienced healing and deliverance at church.

It still happens today. Charlene had been suffering with multiple sclerosis for years and it was getting worse. On one occasion, though she had been able to walk into church that Sunday morning, she suddenly lost all strength in her legs and her friends had to carry her out. But just two months later, in a worship service, she suddenly felt power course through her body and she knew she was healed. She became the most energetic member of her church, leading prayer meetings, chairing committees, and helping others to experience new healing and wholeness in their lives as she had in hers.

Edgar had struggled with alcoholism for a decade. He was newly enrolled in a residential recovery program and one of the requirements was a weekly church service. He had been going to church for several weeks, when the pastor invited people to come forward to pray. Edgar scoffed privately. *The pastor issues an invitation every week, but I've never seen him or any of the church leaders kneel at the front for prayer.* Before he had even completed his thought, the pastor left the pulpit and was one of the first to kneel in prayer. Moments later, Edgar made his way to the front, too. When he finished praying, he was a new man. He has since been sober for more than three decades.

Healing and deliverance can happen in any church. Some churches offer "recovery ministries," helping addicts and others talk openly, deal honestly, and work prayerfully through their struggles. Jim and Amanda Kamisky were helped to recover through Atlanta Outreach, a ministry of North Atlanta Church of Christ:

> "Jimmy had a paper bag with a few clothes in it and the tennis shoes on his feet when I picked him up on the side of the road," [former Atlanta Outreach director Bill] Hale said. Amanda was pregnant with their son, Joey, now eight, and working at a restaurant through a jail work-release program.
>
> After the infant's birth, members cared for Joey while Amanda entered a drug-treatment center. Now, the Kamiskys have good jobs, own a home and rental properties and serve in the recovery ministry.
>
> "It's almost like a fairy tale," she said. "I never dreamed that I would consider church and church people a part of my life. I would never have thought that I would get into a discussion with people at work, talking about God and what the Bible says."[18]

Celebrate Recovery, a national program started in 1991 at Saddleback Church in Lake Forest, California, has helped many find deliverance in and through the church. In addition to dealing with substance abuse, Celebrate Recovery also addresses other compulsive and addictive behaviors, as well as the effects of physical, emotional, and sexual abuse; anger; codependency; and family dysfunction. "I preferred to stay busy with life rather than dealing with life," says Delean, who joined Celebrate Recovery in Austin, Texas. "When I became willing to give God's way a chance, He healed the hurt, shame, guilt, and ugliness of my past. I now understand the freedom a personal relationship with Christ can bring and I found it through honestly working the recovery steps. I now serve as a leader in Celebrate Recovery and it's awesome to watch God use my past to bring hope to others."[19]

As in Lydda back in the days of Peter and Aeneas, so it is today in churches around the world (and in a church near you): God is alive and active among them, healing and delivering, rescuing and restoring broken lives.

"EVERYBODY WHO IS HUMAN HAS SOMETHING TO EXPRESS."
—BRENDA UELAND

CHAPTER 10

EXPRESS

A stately ibex (wild mountain goat), with regal curving horns. Massive mammoths. Running horses with flowing manes. Whole herds of bison and deer. Dancing women. Hunting men. Sun, stars, plants, and human hands.

Those are just some of the artistic depictions found in ancient cave paintings around the world, some of which are estimated to be more than thirty thousand years old.

In 1879, a Spanish nobleman and amateur archaeologist named Marcelino Sanz de Sautuola took his daughter Maria with him to explore a cave near the family estate in northern Spain, about 270 miles north of Madrid. While De Sautuola set about digging in the cave floor, hoping to discover prehistoric bones, tools, or other artifacts, Maria went exploring nearby. Before long, he heard her calling for him. When he responded, she pointed to a section of the cave ceiling depicting surprisingly artistic drawings of a kind of long-extinct cattle called "auruchs." De Sautuola reported the now-famous cave paintings of Altamira, which were so clear and well preserved that experts initially doubted their authenticity. It wasn't until after De Sautuola's death that the paintings were acknowledged to be prehistoric, evidence of Magdalénian culture in southern Europe from what some scientists estimate to be 14,000 to 16,500 years ago.

French school teacher Denis Peyrony had recently visited caves at Les Combarelles with archaeologist Henri Breuil when he explored the cave at Font-de-Gaume (340 miles south of Paris), which was known to locals in the area. There he discovered ancient cave paintings of bison, horses, and mammoths dating to what some estimate to be seventeen thousand years earlier. The cave's most famous painting, however, a frieze of five bison, was discovered in 1966 by scientists who were cleaning the cave. And, though more than two hundred drawings have been discovered, experts believe there are more yet to be uncovered.

In September 1940, four teenagers and a dog discovered a complex network of caves in Lascaux, fifty-five miles east of the Font-de-Gaume cave. Exploring together, they discovered nearly two thousand paintings and carvings of horses, stags, bison, birds, bears, humans, and more. Many of the Lascaux paintings are strikingly sophisticated; some even seem to reveal an understanding of perspective, which would not be systematically applied in Western paintings for another two millennia.

More than three hundred such galleries of ancient drawings, paintings, and carvings have been discovered to date. The Chauvet Cave in southern France and the Cave of El Castillo in northern Spain are the oldest, dating to an estimated thirty thousand and forty thousand years ago, respectively. Cave paintings in Australia are thought to be as old—or older—than that. Some cave paintings are hard to date because they were probably traced or modified over the years. Controversy also surrounds the depictions, as many theories have been put forth about the people who made them—and the purposes they may have served.

But apart from all the "expert" opinions and sometimes fantastical assertions about those prehistoric cave paintings, one thing is certain: They are an example of the need all of us have to express ourselves. It is as true today as it was many thousands of years ago. We want to express ourselves—maybe through painting, sculpture, speech, laughter, dance, or music (in fact, excavations also revealed musical instruments in some of the caves mentioned above).

Author Brenda Ueland wrote,

> Everybody who is human has something to express. Try not expressing anything for twenty-four hours and see what happens. You will nearly explode. You will want to write a long letter or draw a picture or sing or make a dress or plant a garden. Religious men used to go into the wilderness to impose silence on

themselves; but really it was so that they would talk to God. They needed to express something; that is to say, they had thoughts welling up in them and the thoughts went out to someone, whether silently or aloud.[1]

Whether you are an introvert, extrovert, or ambivert, you have something inside you, something to express, a desire to be heard and understood. Like all human beings, you long to speak up and speak out in some way, perhaps verbally, artistically, musically, analytically, electorally, in the spotlight, in the background, even silently. If you are human, you want a voice. You have things to say. You yearn to express yourself. And, if you don't, as Ueland suggests, you are courting disaster. "Unexpressed emotions will never die," said Sigmund Freud. "They are buried alive and will come forth later in uglier ways."[2]

By contrast, the church can help you express your emotions, thoughts, ideas, and abilities in healthy, constructive, and rewarding ways.

Church Can Help You Speak What You Know

Jesus would have recognized the man who asked to meet with him. He wouldn't have missed the significance of the man's visit coming, as it did, after sunset.

The man was a Pharisee—prominent, distinguished—but unlike many of the Pharisees who talked at Jesus, to try to trap Him and trip Him, this man came alone and at night. He had questions. Sincere questions. But he had a reputation to protect; he didn't need the suspicion and ridicule that would result if others in his party learned that he had met with the country rabbi.

Jesus received Nicodemus graciously. He also discerned the genuine interest behind Nicodemus' careful flattery. So Jesus cut to the chase: "Listen, if you want to see the kingdom of God, you must be born again."

Nicodemus leaned forward. He was fully engaged, but confused. "What do you mean?" he said. "No one can return to his mother's womb and be born again."

"I am not speaking in natural terms; I am speaking of the supernatural. Don't act surprised when I say, 'You must be born again.' Take the wind, for example. It blows here and there, and you can hear it—but you don't know where it comes from or where it goes; it's a mystery. Just like this new birth."

But Nicodemus still didn't get it, though he was a highly respected scholar among his people.

That's when Jesus said, "We speak what we know and what we have seen, and you still struggle to understand. How will you manage if I tell you even loftier things—the whole mind-blowing truth? But I will put it as simply as I can: Just as Moses raised up the bronze snake on a pole in the wilderness, so will the Son of Man be lifted up, so that anyone who believes in Him will have eternal life."[3]

Jesus told Nicodemus, "We speak what we know and what we have seen." Up until that time, he had used the pronouns "I" and "you." But He shifted suddenly and said, "We speak what we know and what we have seen." The plural is noteworthy, because He is not just speaking of Himself, but of "everyone who is born of the Spirit."[4]

In other words, Jesus said that those who are born of the Spirit speak...what they know. They express what they have inside them, for (as Jesus said elsewhere), "the mouth speaks what the heart is full of."[5] Such expression is a natural—and often supernatural—overflow of what God has done and is doing in a person's heart and life.

The early account of the church's history bears this out. When God's Spirit overtook the first church in Jerusalem on the day of Pentecost (as recorded in Acts 2 and described earlier in this book), Peter stood up and addressed the crowd of thousands that had gathered to see what was going on. Peter, the Galilean fisherman who, up to that time, had been known mostly as someone who leapt before looking and struck before thinking. Not only was he not a persuasive speaker, he was clearly afflicted with foot-in-mouth disease. Yet, on that very first day of the church's existence, he spoke eloquently and effectively to a sizeable crowd which he would go on to do repeatedly. It wasn't just Peter who found his voice in the church, though. Philip, it turns out, apparently discovered a penchant for teaching cross-culturally.[6] Paul and Barnabas learned that they had a knack for speaking to Gentiles rather than Jews.[7]

Since then, millions upon millions have fulfilled Jesus' words, "We speak what we know and what we have seen." Some churches encourage worshipers to "share a word" or "give a testimony" as part of the worship experience itself. One person may simply give thanks for waking up that morning in good health, while others may speak at length about how God's power has changed their lives. Many churches offer classes on how to share your faith with others. Some pastors and teachers help new Christians write out the story of how they experienced new life in Christ, which can help prepare them to tell the story more readily when the opportunity presents itself.

You may not be comfortable speaking in front of others, but that doesn't mean you can't speak what you know. Many shy or reserved followers of Jesus have expressed themselves in writing or in one-on-one settings. Some have found great fulfillment in quietly, but courageously, taking a stand for what they know and what they have experienced.

One such person was Rosa Parks, who has been called the mother of the civil rights movement in the United States. When the forty-two-year-old seamstress and deaconess in her church refused to give up her seat on a crowded Montgomery, Alabama, bus in 1955, she drew upon her deep faith and her sense of "Christian responsibility to act."[8]

There are things inside you that deserve to be expressed. Even if you never make a speech or give a sermon, the church can be a place that helps you find—and refine—your voice.

Church Can Help You Express Yourself Artistically

Who do you think is the first person the Bible describes as being "filled" with the Spirit of God? Who would be your first guess? Adam, the first man, who was created in perfect innocence and beauty? Who walked with God in the fresh morning dew of the Garden of Eden? Who dwelt in unbroken, untainted intimacy with the Creator?

Or maybe Noah, who was uniquely favored by God in his generation? Noah, who obeyed God's instruction to build a boat that would preserve human and animal life on an otherwise doomed planet? Noah, who was the first person in history to see a rainbow, the sign of God's promise never to flood the whole earth again?

Perhaps Abraham, the friend of God? The one who left his home for a distant country and an uncertain future because God told him to?

Isaac? Jacob? Joseph? Moses?

How about none of the above?

No, the first person described in the Bible as being filled with the Spirit is probably someone you have never heard of before. His name was Bezalel and he was an artist:

> Then the Lord said to Moses, "See, I have chosen Bezalel son of Uri, the son of Hur, of the tribe of Judah, and I have filled him with the Spirit of God, with wisdom, with understanding, with knowledge and with all kinds of skills—to make artistic designs for work in gold, silver and bronze, to cut and set stones, to work in wood, and to engage in all kinds of crafts. Moreover, I have appointed Oholiab son of Ahisamak, of the tribe of Dan, to help him. Also I have given ability to all the skilled workers to make everything I have commanded you: the tent of meeting, the ark of the covenant law with the atonement cover on it, and all the other furnishings of the tent—the table and its articles, the pure gold lampstand and all its accessories, the altar of incense, the altar of burnt offering and all its utensils, the basin with its stand—and also the woven garments, both the sacred garments for Aaron the priest and the garments for his sons when they serve as priests, and the anointing oil and fragrant incense for the Holy Place. They are to make them just as I commanded you."[9]

Not only was Bezalel filled with the Spirit of God, but his name has been preserved for thirty-five hundred years as someone who expressed himself artistically among God's people. He applied his skills to the construction of the tabernacle in the wilderness. He made artistic designs, accessories, and furnishings for ancient Israel's place of worship. He was the first of a long line of gifted artists and craftsman who have expressed themselves through the company of God's people.

You may be one of Bezalel's heirs who finds a place to express yourself giftedly in the church. Yours may be a visual or spatial gift, like Bezalel's, that can find its full expression in the church, among God's people. You may be a sculptor or a painter. You may be a master carpenter, skilled in handling wood. You may be a potter, who can create works of art in ceramics.

Of course, you may express yourself in other ways—musically, perhaps. Through singing, songwriting, playing an instrument, or conducting a chorus or ensemble you may find your heart's best expression. Or maybe by clapping or playing a tambourine while others are singing.

You may be one of Lydia's heirs. She was a wealthy dealer in textiles who hosted missionaries in her home.[10] Like her, you may find your "voice" in quilting, selling, or showing hospitality to others.

You may share Tabitha's gift of making treasured articles of clothing for widows and other people in need. You may find your soul's expression in cooking or baking. Or perhaps you express yourself in worshipful forms of dance or in teaching others to dance. Or in writing. Or in drama. Or directing video productions.

Take Diane for instance. When she first started to follow Jesus, she thought she had little to offer in service to the church. She had no musical ability. She was terrified of public speaking. She had no talent for teaching. But one Sunday morning she came to church with a small flower arrangement she had put together from her garden and she asked the pastor if she could place it on the piano in the church auditorium. Soon, people were asking about the beautiful bouquet and she became the unofficial flower arranger for the church. Before long, she had another idea; she created a garden, with a functioning fountain, on the platform for the church's worship services leading up to and including Easter. Next, the pastor approached her about creating a banner to hang in the auditorium during the Christmas season, which added so much beauty to the room that she continued the practice, creating a new banner every month or two.

Many people have discovered what Diane learned: There are many ways for people like her—and Bezalel, Lydia, and Tabitha—to express what is inside them, in ways that will help the church and bless countless others.

Church Can Help You Share Your Life

Not everyone is artistic, or musical, of course. Or even bold enough to speak out. But everyone has something inside them...something worth expressing...something that cries out to be shared.

Paul, the great church planter of the first century, referred to it when he wrote to the church in a town called Thessalonica:

> You know, brothers and sisters, that our visit to you was not without results. We had previously suffered and been treated outrageously in Philippi, as you know, but with the help of our God we dared to tell you his gospel in the face of strong opposition. For the appeal we make does not spring from error or impure motives, nor are we trying to trick you. On the contrary, we speak as those approved by God to be entrusted with the gospel. We are not trying to please people but God, who tests our hearts. You know we never used flattery, nor did we put on a mask to cover up greed—God is our witness. We were not looking for praise from people, not from you or anyone else, even though as apostles of Christ we could have asserted our authority. Instead, we were like young children among you.
>
> Just as a nursing mother cares for her children, so

we cared for you. Because we loved you so much, we were delighted to share with you not only the gospel of God but our lives as well. [11]

Paul and his traveling companions shared the gospel—the good news that Jesus Christ had died for the sins of the world and offered forgiveness and new life to all—but they had something else to share, he said: "our lives as well."

That is, Paul and his church-planting team suffered with people when they suffered. They laughed at each other's jokes. They ate together. They cared for each other, like a nursing mother cares for her children. They loved each other. They loved each other's children. They shared their lives.

The church offers a golden opportunity for self-expression, even for those who think they have little to offer. Because there has probably never been a greater need than there is today—in our age of social isolation and alienation—for people who are willing to share their lives with others, to figure out new ways to care for others, and even to resurrect old ways of connecting with others.

For example, you may feel a little nervous about walking into church by yourself and sitting by yourself, but think about this: Chances are, when you walk into church and look for a place to sit, there will be someone in that room sitting all alone. You may not know that person, you may never have laid eyes on him or her before. What if you decided, instead of feeling nervous about sitting by yourself, to look for someone sitting all alone and sit with that person? You can leave a little space between the two of you, of course, but you may be surprised at the mutual comfort and blessing you can express by just sitting near someone else— and maybe exchanging a nod and a smile. It is a small thing, but it is one way to share your life with another.

A cultural custom that has largely disappeared in the last couple of generations is the practice of inviting others into our homes to share a meal. What if you went a step further than sitting near someone in church and actually looked for people to invite to lunch after church? You may feel awkward at first, particularly if you have only a nodding acquaintance with someone. You may have to ask more than once before your invitation is accepted, but you may also be surprised at the new friendships that can develop if you're willing to take the initiative in sharing your life with others.

Here is just one more idea: regardless of how young or old you are, there are likely to be people in any church who haven't experienced the same things you have—and who might be grateful for some help or guidance in what they are facing. Just as Barnabas "took [Saul] under his wing"[12] and became a mentor to the man who had recently met the risen Jesus on the road to Damascus, there may be someone in your church who could use a little coaching. You may have business experience that someone might find useful. You may tutor someone who is struggling in school. You could help someone learn how to change the oil in his or her car. You may not have the spiritual depth or background that Barnabas did, but there are multiple ways to share your life with others, wherever you may be in your spiritual journey.

These are just suggestions. If they don't resonate with you, it may be because there are better ways to express yourself—ways that are more particular to you as a person. Ways that fulfill your need to be heard and understood, to speak up and speak out. Ways to let what is *inside* you overflow *from* you. Ways to say what you want your life to say. Ways that reflect who you are and what God has done—or is doing—for you, in you, and through you.

The church can give you the opportunity to say that.

To sing it.

To share it.

"THINK WHERE MAN'S GLORY MOST BEGINS AND ENDS, AND SAY MY GLORY WAS I HAD SUCH FRIENDS."

—WILLIAM BUTLER YEATS

CHAPTER 11

FLOURISH

It was started by a Harvard sophomore. He had already created something called Facemash, posting photos of his fellow students side by side on a web page, and inviting visitors to the site to vote on who was more attractive. Facemash attracted a lot of traffic and got its creator into trouble. Harvard administrators shut it down and threatened the student, Mark Zuckerberg, with expulsion.

However, Zuckerberg was undeterred. The next semester he began writing computer code for a new website, and launched "thefacebook" on February 4, 2004. Similar to college "facebooks," which were photo directories put together for incoming first-year students, "thefacebook" expanded on the idea by allowing participants to post other information and to comment back and forth with each other.

At first, "thefacebook" was restricted to Harvard students (and within the first month, more than half had joined the site). A month later, the site became available to students at Stanford, Columbia, and Yale, and continued to expand to include other Ivy League schools—and then most of the universities in the United States and Canada. In 2006, Facebook became available to anyone age thirteen or older with a valid e-mail address.

After that, of course, it became an international phenomenon, giving people the opportunity to reconnect with old friends, make new friends, and communicate with friends regardless of the geographical distance between them. Facebook even spawned new words and terms, such as "Facebook friends," "friended," and "unfriended." In fact, in 2010, *The Oxford English Dictionary* added the word friend as a verb for the first time, meaning to add someone to your list of acquaintances on Facebook (depending on the level of privacy you choose, only people you approve as "friends" can see all of your information, photos, and posts, or updates, on Facebook).

Facebook friends may include childhood playmates, long-lost classmates, family members, business associates, passing acquaintances, and even people you've never met—perhaps even some you'd never want to meet. Facebook allows busy people to feel connected with other human beings in the course of a day, week, or month, even if they've never left their house—or their desk.

There are limits to Facebook's usefulness, however. It can introduce you to new people, and many use it to get and stay connected with friends, but it is no substitute for the kinds of friendships that can be found, cultivated, and deepened by means of involvement in a good church, friendships that can help you flourish and thrive.

Church Can Introduce You to Praying Friends

You may not believe in prayer. You may not be convinced that it makes a difference. You may even think it is a waste of time, time that could be better spent on other things.

But even if all of that is true of you, there may still be times in your life when you wouldn't mind knowing that someone is praying for you. Even if you're not sure it would do any good, it might still be nice to know that there are people in your life who think of you whether you're around or not, who care enough to devote their precious time to praying for you, and who are willing to ask God to help you and bless you.

Where do you find friends like that? The answer should be obvious: You will find that kind of friend in church. Peter did in the early church in Jerusalem. Peter is basically the main character throughout the first chapters of the book of Acts in the Bible. Acts describes him repeatedly getting in trouble with the religious and civil authorities because he boldly and publicly preached about the crucified—and risen—Jesus Christ in the city where Jesus had been arrested, tried, and executed (and where some of the people who had participated in it were still not only alive but in power). So he (and others, like John) were regularly arrested, imprisoned, and beaten. Through it all, though, notice what the Bible account says:

On their release, Peter and John went back to their own people and reported all that the chief priests and the elders had said to them. When they heard this, they raised their voices together in prayer to God.[1]

So Peter was kept in prison, but the church was earnestly praying to God for him.[2]

He went to the house of Mary the mother of John, also called Mark, where many people had gathered and were praying.[3]

Wouldn't it be nice to know that, wherever you are and whatever you are going through, your friends are praying for you? That is one of the greatest blessings that come from being part of a church. And it isn't confined to those times when you are in need or in trouble. In one of his letters, the apostle Paul concluded by relaying greetings to the church from someone in his traveling party, saying, "Epaphras, who is one of you and a servant of Christ Jesus, sends greetings. He is always wrestling in prayer for you."[4] Every church has someone—or more than one—like that. People *wrestle* in prayer for others. There are folks you can call on at a moment's notice. And friends will pray for you and your well-being through bad times, good times, and in-between times.

Church Can Acquaint You with Giving Friends

Molly and Paul, a young couple who were given one week to switch apartments (at a time when Molly was pregnant with their second child), were overwhelmed on moving day until a dozen people from church showed up to help them load, unload, and clean.

Lynn and Mike have received several envelopes of cash in their mailbox from an anonymous source. The money is given in such a way that they can't refuse it or repay it, but they're confident that it comes from someone (or several "someones") in their prayer group at church.

Tonya heard her pastor tell the story one Sunday in church of a man who had given away numerous cars and trucks to people in need. When the service concluded, she told the pastor that she had a pressing need for a car, but no money to buy one. An hour later, the pastor introduced her to a couple in the church who wanted to give away their car...to her.

Molly, Paul, Lynn, Mike, and Tonya belong to the same church in the midwestern United States. It is not a large church. There are no rich people in the church. But like many, it is a church of many giving people. Like those described in the fourth chapter of the book of Acts:

> There were no needy persons among them. For from time to time those who owned land or houses sold them, brought the money from the sales and put it at the apostles' feet, and it was distributed to anyone who had need.
>
> Joseph, a Levite from Cyprus, whom the apostles called Barnabas (which means "son of encouragement"), sold a field he owned and brought the money and put it at the apostles' feet.[5]

No one is suggesting that you should participate in a church in order to receive gifts of land, houses, and money. However, when you become involved in a healthy church, you will soon enjoy the friendship of giving people like those who blessed Molly and Paul, Lynn and Mike, and Tonya. You may be surprised by friends who would loan you their pickup truck or their chainsaw, who would drive you back and forth to your chemo treatments, and even give you their blood...or their box seat tickets to the ball game.

Church Can Equip You with Supportive Friends

You remember Saul from previous chapters, of course—the man who persecuted the early church and then unexpectedly met the risen Jesus Christ on the road to Damascus. You remember how he waited three days in Damascus until a man named Ananias called on him, healed his blindness, and baptized him, but there is more to that part of Saul's story:

> Saul spent several days with the disciples in Damascus. At once he began to preach in the synagogues that Jesus is the Son of God. All those who heard him were astonished and asked, "Isn't he the man who raised havoc in Jerusalem among those who call on this name? And hasn't he come here to take them as prisoners to the chief priests?" Yet Saul grew more and more powerful and baffled the Jews living in Damascus by proving that Jesus is the Messiah.
>
> After many days had gone by, there was a conspiracy among the Jews to kill him, but Saul learned of their plan. Day and night they kept close watch on the city gates in order to kill him. But his followers took him by night and lowered him in a basket through an opening in the wall.[6]

We don't know how many days, weeks, or months Saul spent in Damascus. We do know that, by the time he left town, he had made friends there who would support him (quite literally, in fact) and help him escape a plot on his life.

You, too, can expect to find supportive friendships in the church. Friends who will listen. Friends who will notice when you're feeling down. Friends who will visit you when you're sick. Friends you can call when you get bad news. People who will pitch in when you need a hand, and who will comfort and defend you when others conspire and attack.

Church Can Bless You with Mentoring Friends

When you were growing up, there were people in your life who taught you, coached you, and helped you become the person you are today. An early teacher maybe took a special interest in you and spent extra time with you when you started to fall behind. An older sibling might have shown you the ropes, and maybe even taken your punishment at times. Perhaps a coach could have left you on the bench, but took the time instead to practice, practice, practice with you.

You may have gotten to where you are today solely on your own, but chances are, someone helped you and coached you along the way. That person was a mentor to you.

Unfortunately, as we get older, we lose our mentors. We fail to enlist new ones. Sometimes we forget that new situations and new challenges call for the development of new skills, and that no matter how successful we have been in the past, there is almost always someone around who can share valuable wisdom and expertise to speed our improvement and deepen our development.

The church offers tremendous opportunities for the development of mentoring friendships, as illustrated not only in Paul's relationship with Barnabas (mentioned in chapter eight), but also in Paul's later relationship with a man named Timothy:

> Paul came to Derbe and then to Lystra, where a disciple named Timothy lived, whose mother was Jewish and a believer but whose father was a Greek. The believers at Lystra and Iconium spoke well of him. Paul wanted to take him along on the journey, so he circumcised him because of the Jews who lived in that area, for they all knew that his father was a Greek. As they traveled from town to town, they delivered the decisions reached by the apostles and elders in Jerusalem for the people to obey. So the churches were strengthened in the faith and grew daily in numbers.[7]

Timothy found a life-changing mentor in Paul, the great planter of first-century churches. Timothy not only began traveling with Paul and learning from him, but he also eventually became the pastor of what may have been Paul's favorite church, in Ephesus. And, thanks to Paul's productive mentoring of Timothy, the church today has two extremely instructive letters to Timothy—First Timothy and Second Timothy—which are part of the Bible.

Finding a mentoring friend these days won't get your name

etched in church history and included prominently in the pages of the Bible, but you may be surprised at how much the church can bless you in that respect. With the help of a mentor she met in church, Stacy learned to manage her business account. With the help of a mentor, Bill became a better guitarist. With the help of a mentor, Dan got pretty good at laying tile. Greg took his first steps as a preacher. Jenn got her blog up and running. With the help of a mentor, Carl started the exercise program that helped him lose ninety pounds...and may have saved his life.

You may already know how to do all those things. But no matter how old or how skilled you are, there are probably still plenty of things a mentoring friend can teach you, coach you, and help you develop, not only spiritually but in all other ways as well.

Church Can Introduce You to a Healing Friend

It must be acknowledged, at this point, that becoming involved in a good church is not without its risks. We don't need to read any further than the account of Paul preaching in the port city of Troas to become aware of that:

> On the first day of the week, we gathered with the local believers to share in the Lord's Supper. Paul was preaching to them, and since he was leaving the next day, he kept talking until midnight. The upstairs room where we met was lighted with many flickering lamps. As Paul spoke on and on, a young man named Eutychus, sitting on the windowsill, became very drowsy. Finally, he fell sound asleep and dropped three stories to his death below. Paul went down, bent over him, and took him into his arms. "Don't worry," he said, "he's alive!" Then they all went back upstairs, shared in the Lord's Supper, and ate together. Paul continued talking to them until dawn, and then he left. Meanwhile, the young man was taken home unhurt, and everyone was greatly relieved.[8]

There are, of course, several lessons that could be drawn from that passage (1. Before the sermon starts, make sure your fall will be cushioned!). One way to apply those verses is to note how relieved and grateful Eutychus and the others would have been that their circle of friends included someone who (though he could apparently talk a person to death!) was a healing friend.

The most important application of that passage, however, is to remind you that whatever you may need healing from, the church today still can introduce you to the One who has the power to heal your spirit, soul, and body.

Church Can Furnish You with Fast Friends

One of the many downsides to our frenzied, fractured society in the twenty-first century is that it has become harder in recent generations to develop the kind of deep, abiding friendships that used to sustain people and enrich their lives. While much of our lifestyle seems to prevent deep and meaningful friendships, the church still offers opportunities to develop steadfast friendships, like those reflected in the scene of the apostle Paul's emotional farewell with his friends in the Ephesian church.

Paul had started the church at Ephesus, spending more time developing the church in that city than in any other. Later, he assigned his protégé Timothy to oversee that church.[9] Though the leaders of the church had probably been selected by Timothy, they were probably people Paul had converted and mentored. So when Paul sensed God's Spirit telling him to go to Jerusalem, despite the likelihood of persecution and imprisonment, he made sure that his itinerary included a stop at the port of Miletus, near Ephesus. Upon arriving at Miletus, he sent a message to the church in Ephesus, asking for his friends to travel there to meet with him.

When they arrived, he explained where he was headed, and why. He reminded them of their shared past. He told them they would probably never see his face again. He gave them some final words of encouragement and urged them to stay strong. Acts 20 describes their parting:

When Paul had finished speaking, he knelt down with all of them and prayed. They all wept as they embraced him and kissed him. What grieved them most was his statement that they would never see his face again. Then they accompanied him to the ship.[10]

It is a moving portrayal of fast friends saying goodbye, and a depiction of the kind of deep, steadfast friendships that many people enjoy because of the church. They got involved, they made friends, they served God together, they endured hardship together and, day by day and month by month, they grew closer and deeper and stronger in their love for one another.

Those steadfast friendships are increasingly rare in today's world, but they can still be found—and are, in fact, still common—in the church.

Church Can Give You an Extended Network of Friends

When Paul warned his Ephesian friends that they wouldn't see him again, he was telling the truth. He was arrested in Jerusalem and imprisoned. He escaped an assassination plot and endured multiple court trials. Finally, he was shipped off to Rome, the capital of the Empire, for trial before Caesar. It was an eventful journey, which is described in Acts 27 and 28, and begins with this detail:

> When it was decided that we would sail for Italy, Paul and some other prisoners were handed over to a centurion named Julius, who belonged to the Imperial Regiment. We boarded a ship from Adramyttium about to sail for ports along the coast of the province of Asia, and we put out to sea. Aristarchus, a Macedonian from Thessalonica, was with us.
>
> The next day we landed at Sidon; and Julius, in kindness to Paul, allowed him to go to his friends so they might provide for his needs. From there we put out to sea again and passed to the lee of Cyprus because the winds were against us.[11]

The verses that follow describe storms and shipwreck and snakebites. By comparison, the account of the journey's beginning is mundane. It might make a person wonder why the author bothered to include it. One reason might be the mention of the stopover at Sidon, where "Julius, in kindness to Paul, allowed him to go to his friends so they might provide for his needs."[12] It is significant, especially in light of the passage we just encountered about Paul's reunion with his friends from Ephesus at the port of Miletus, because it is a matter-of-fact depiction of the fellowship of the church around the world. From his many travels and his long, hard labors, Paul probably had friends in most ports in the civilized world, so to find friends in Sidon would have been no surprise.

However, the same is true of people in churches almost anywhere you go today. Ben has always lived in Dallas, but through his church, he has friends in Denver, Toronto, Los Angeles, Syracuse, and Minneapolis, among other places. Georgetta's church belongs to an association of churches that gets together four times a year, so she has made numerous friends throughout a four-state area. Travis is serving his second stint in the U.S. Navy, but in almost any port or place he has visited, he has found a church similar to his home church in Cincinnati. So although he may be a world away from home, when he enters a church he feels right at home. When a person experiences new life in Christ and unites with the church, he or she becomes part of an extended family—a worldwide family. Wherever he or she may go, there will be brothers and sisters in Christ waiting to be discovered.

Church Can Cheer You with Encouraging Friends

Paul's final journey, described in the book of Acts, finally approached its destination—after many twists and turns (and typhoons!) along the way. But even after detours and shipwreck, the last legs of the trip contained a few more surprises:

> After three months we put out to sea in a ship that had wintered in the island—it was an Alexandrian

ship with the figurehead of the twin gods Castor and Pollux. We put in at Syracuse and stayed there three days. From there we set sail and arrived at Rhegium. The next day the south wind came up, and on the following day we reached Puteoli. There we found some brothers and sisters who invited us to spend a week with them. And so we came to Rome. The brothers and sisters there had heard that we were coming, and they traveled as far as the Forum of Appius and the Three Taverns to meet us. At the sight of these people Paul thanked God and was encouraged.[13]

Paul had never been to Rome. He had never been to Syracuse or Rhegium or Puteoli. But even so, there were followers of Jesus who, when they heard that Paul and his traveling party (which included Luke, the author of Acts) were coming, they took the time to go out to meet them and even invite Paul's entourage to spend a week with them. It was a gesture and a sight that "encouraged Paul" and prompted him to give thanks to God.

Of course it did. It will do the same for you, when you experience the encouragement the church can give to a weary heart. You can experience the hospitality of people you've just met who want to show you kindness. And you can experience the kind of friendships that make you want to give thanks to God.

They won't come right away, of course, nor all at once, but imagine how different things will be for you as those kinds of friendships are added to your life. Praying friends. Giving friendships. Mentoring, supporting, and healing friendships. Steadfast. Extensive. Deep. Encouraging.

"WE MUST LAY ONE BRICK AT A TIME, TAKE ONE STEP AT A TIME."

—DOROTHY DAY

CHAPTER 12

START

Some consider them to be the most famous words in sports. The Grand Marshal of NASCAR Sprint Cup Series races usually opens the races with the words, "Gentlemen, start your engines."

But for the first time ever, a woman—Danica Patrick—was starting a Cup race from the coveted pole position. So actor James Franco (*Spiderman, 127 Hours, Oz the Great and Powerful*), in his role as Grand Marshal of the 2013 Daytona 500, started the race with the words, "Drivers...and Danica...start your engines!"

Franco sparked a controversy, not just because he had changed the famous formula (some of Patrick's previous races had begun with "Lady and gentlemen, start your engines"), but also for the awkward phrasing that distinguished Patrick, not from "gentlemen" but from "drivers."

Still, it was a historic occasion. And, though it may not have begun perfectly, the race did begin.

There is a lesson in that.

The author of the ancient book of Ecclesiastes, which is attributed to King Solomon, said, "If you wait for perfect conditions, you will never get anything done."[1] If you wait for the perfect weather to plant your seeds, you'll never enjoy a bountiful harvest. If you wait for inspiration to strike, you'll never get your book written. If you wait until you can "afford" to have children, you'll never start a family. And if you wait for the ideal moment to become involved in church, you will never quite get around to enjoying all the benefits this book has discussed.

So don't wait. Don't delay. Don't procrastinate. When Joshua prepared the people of Israel to cross the Jordan River and enter their Promised Land, he instructed them to follow the priests, who were to carry the Ark of the Covenant at the head of the procession. The priests were instructed to step into the river's water. Only after the priests got their feet wet did the waters part, allowing everyone else to cross "on dry ground."[2] Sometimes you just have to get your feet wet. You have to take a step of faith. You have to stop waiting for perfect conditions. Even if the call to action seems awkward and imperfect, get going.

Hang In

Sometimes stories and incidents in the Bible seem too short, even incomplete. For example, the book of Acts tells us about Philip meeting the Ethiopian official on the Gaza road, an encounter that culminated in the Ethiopian's baptism, but wouldn't it be nice to know the rest of the story? For example, what became of the Ethiopian after he returned to his home country?

Or what about Saul's traveling companions on the road to Damascus? Were they affected in any way by the blinding light and the voice from heaven that Saul heard? Were any of them influenced by Saul's "defection" to the other side? Did they just drop off Saul in Damascus and go on about their business of persecuting Christians? We can trust that if such things were essential information, they would have been recorded. But still, it would be nice to know.

One more example: Remember when Saul's friends in Damascus helped him escape a plot on his life by lowering him in a basket through an opening in the city wall?[3] Luke, the author of Acts, tells us quite matter-of-factly how he made his escape, but it would be nice to know if, as he dangled from the wall in a basket, any of his friends urged him to "hang in there!"

Probably not. Those first-century Damascenes may have had a different sense of humor than we do today. Whether it was said or not—and whether anyone would have thought it even mildly humorous—we know that Saul *did* hang in there. Even when within weeks of his encounter with Jesus, he was threatened and hunted by his former allies.[4] Even though, when he arrived in Jerusalem, he initially met skepticism and suspicion from the church.[5] And when the authorities in Jerusalem tried to kill him, causing his new friends in the church to ship him off to his hometown, Tarsus.[6] He didn't give up. He hung in there.

So should you. Even if you hit a few bumps in the road. Even if conditions are less than perfect, hang in there.

Move forward from wherever you are right now. Don't feel like you have to have everything figured out. Don't think that you need to know your way around, either physically or spiritually. You don't. Just move forward from wherever you are now. If that's a place of doubt and uncertainty, just keep moving forward. If you're in a place of reluctance, keep moving forward. If you feel spiritually dull or inert, move onward. If you're on a high or at a low, move ahead.

Take things a step at a time. Like the priests carrying the Ark of the Covenant across the Jordan River, start by stepping into things. Put one foot in front of the other. Take things one at a time. You may be tempted to jump in with both feet or to dive in headfirst, getting involved in everything the church offers and drinking in all the benefits. But you will probably be better off to take a more measured approach. Observe. Enjoy. Just don't try to do everything at once, especially if you have not been involved in the church before (or for a long time). Start by attending worship every week, and progress forward from there, one step at a time.

Ask questions. Most of us become reluctant to ask questions during our school years; we are afraid others will think we are unintelligent, and perhaps even make fun of us. Therefore, we learn to keep our mouths shut and refrain from asking questions. But church is not first grade. Though worship services are not usually constructed to allow for questions and answers, there is no taboo against asking questions at other times. In fact, most pastors and church leaders love to answer questions ranging from "What does that word you keep using mean?" to "Why don't the words in my Bible match the words the pastor reads aloud?" and so on.

Be patient. When the Jerusalem church got started, everyone was amazed and enthusiastic. It was exciting, but it was a work in progress. There were plenty of opportunities for those first church folk to exercise patience. Like when the Greek-speaking widows started feeling neglected.[7] Or when the church's leaders weren't sure exactly how to handle non-Jewish people who were joining the church.[8] The church today is no different. You may slide right into the life of your church like Cinderella putting on her glass slipper; or you may have a little bit of trial-and-error ahead of you as you become more and more familiar with your church. Either way is okay. Just be patient, and give yourself and others time to learn, adjust, and get comfortable.

Don't expect perfection. There is no perfect church. There weren't even any perfect churches in biblical times. They all had problems. They all had difficulties. Mainly because they all had people in them, and people are all imperfect. So don't be surprised if you meet some of those imperfect people and they get on your nerves. If that happens, just try to remember two things: (1) The church exists for imperfect people; and, (2) You are one of them!

Join In

In the earliest days of church history, the church was made up of all kinds of people, many of whom you've already met in the preceding pages of this book. Peter and John, a couple of Galilean fishermen, were two of the early leaders. And Mary, the mother of Jesus,[9] of course. There were also Jewish priests in the mix.[10] An Ethiopian government official.[11] Saul, a Pharisee.[12] Cornelius, a Roman centurion.[13] Lydia, a wealthy businesswoman.[14] Dionysius, a high-ranking judge in Athens.[15] Even members of Caesar's household in Rome.[16] Such a diverse assortment of people.

The churches themselves were diverse, too. The church in Jerusalem was the first church in history. The church in Antioch (in what is now Syria) was where followers of Jesus were first called Christians, and apparently the first church to intentionally send out a team of missionaries. The church in Berea was characterized by careful Bible study; and the church in Corinth seemed always to have more problems than solutions.

The same is true today. Churches are like snowflakes; no

two are identical. Every church has its unique advantages and challenges. Churches also differ in how they include people and integrate them into the life of the church. So, while it is always a good idea to consult the pastors and leaders of your church for more specific guidance, the following steps are offered to help you not only *hang* in there in getting to know your church better, but also to take the next steps to *join in.*

Receive the gift of salvation. When Jesus met Nicodemus late one night in Jerusalem, He explained to the Pharisee that high-sounding words and religious platitudes could never help a person enter the kingdom of God. Jesus said, "Very truly I tell you, no one can see the kingdom of God unless they are born again."[17] Nicodemus had apparently never heard things explained in such terms, so he asked Jesus for clarification. Jesus answered, "Flesh gives birth to flesh, but the Spirit gives birth to spirit. You should not be surprised at my saying, 'You must be born again.' The wind blows wherever it pleases. You hear its sound, but you cannot tell where it comes from or where it is going. So it is with everyone born of the Spirit."[18] He went on to refer to His fast-approaching crucifixion:

> "Just as Moses lifted up the snake in the wilderness, so the Son of Man must be lifted up, that everyone who believes may have eternal life in him.
>
> "For God so loved the world that he gave his one and only Son, that whoever believes in him shall not perish but have eternal life. For God did not send his Son into the world to condemn the world, but to save the world through him."[19]

According to Jesus, then, the way to enter the kingdom of God is not by joining a church. It's exactly the reverse. The way to join the church is by entering the kingdom of God. The first and most important step is, in the words of Jesus, "Be born again." And the way to do that is to believe in Jesus—not merely to believe that he existed, or even that he died for the sins of the world, but to believe him, to trust him, to place your faith in him and surrender your life to him as your Savior from guilt, sin, and death, and as the controlling influence of your life. That can happen by sincerely praying a simple prayer—if you pray it wholeheartedly. If you haven't taken that step before now, would you take a moment, quiet your heart, focus your mind, and pray the following?

> "Lord Jesus, I need You. Thank You for dying on the cross for my sins. I open the door of my life and receive You as my Savior and Lord. Thank You for forgiving my sins and giving me eternal life. Take control of my life from this moment on, and make me the kind of person You want me to be."

If you have honestly and sincerely prayed that prayer, the Bible says that you have passed from death to life, from darkness to light, and from the power of Satan to the kingdom of God. Also, according to the Bible, you have simultaneously received forgiveness of sins and membership in the mystical, worldwide church. But that doesn't mean you've done all you can do and received all the blessings that are available to you.

Get baptized. When John the Baptist began preaching in the wilderness to prepare people for the coming of Jesus the Messiah, Jews (like John and all his audience at that time) observed a custom called the mikvah, a ritual bath that cleansed people so they could worship God. John introduced a new concept, though: baptism for repentance (that is, being immersed in water to signify your sorrow for your sins and your intention to live differently in the future). Once the church was born, the practice of baptism was seen in a new light, as an indicator not only that a person was forgiven, but also that "the old life is gone; a new life has begun!"[20]

In fact, in a circular letter to several churches, Paul once wrote, "in Christ Jesus you are all children of God through faith. As many of you as were baptized into Christ have clothed yourselves with Christ."[21] He assumed that the person who is a child of God through faith in Jesus Christ would be baptized. He equated baptism with new life in Jesus Christ. So, if you are such a person—if you change your mind regarding (repent of) your sins and surrender your life to Jesus as your Savior from guilt, sin, and death, and as the controlling influence of your life—then the next thing to do is to be baptized. Your pastor will be thrilled to help you take that step. And, to make sure that it is as meaningful and powerful a demonstration of your faith in Jesus Christ as possible, consider the following:

> 1. *Make it a celebration.* Some churches have baptismal tanks or pools inside the church auditorium, allowing you to be baptized as part of a weekend worship celebration. Other churches schedule baptisms in lakes, ponds, or rivers. Some even host baptism pool parties in church members' swimming pools. Whatever your church's custom is, cooperate with your pastor and other church leaders to make it a joyful celebration of your faith in Christ.

> 2. *Make it a witness.* Many of your church friends and family will, of course, want to celebrate your baptism with you. But don't neglect to invite people who haven't yet experienced new life in Christ. In fact, one of the interesting characteristics of the book of Acts is the fact that three separate times, the author (Luke) relates the story of the apostle Paul's conversion. Three times in the same book. You might think Luke would have told the story and then subsequently summarized it. Luke didn't do that, though. He recorded the story three separate times. Why? Maybe because he knew that the story of Paul's turnaround would have a powerful effect on those who read it or heard it. The same is true of your story. Even if you're too shy to say much at your baptism, the act itself can be a powerful way to show others what has happened in your life. So think of all the people you would invite to, say, a milestone birthday party; there is no good reason not to invite them to a baptism as well. Family, friends, coworkers, classmates, and neighbors can all be invited to your baptism, which is most meaningful when it signifies your experience of new life in Christ to the important people of your life.

3. *Make it a "line in the sand."* When God's people in the ancient world reached a significant juncture in their journey, they would often build an altar to mark that moment. Noah did it after the flood. Jacob did it after his dream at Bethel. Joshua did it after crossing the Jordan into the Promised Land. Consider making your baptism a similar epochal event, a demarcation between the old and the new, a watershed moment in your life that reminds you, from that point onward, "The old life is gone; a new life has begun!"[22]

4. *Commit to membership.* Different churches also handle membership differently. In some churches, the pastor invites people at the end of a worship service to join the church. Other churches host classes so prospective members can learn more about the opportunities, privileges, and responsibilities of membership in the church. Whatever it looks like in your church, don't just hang around. Keep moving forward, take a step at a time, be patient...but pursue becoming a part of the body, a fully committed and fully functioning member of the church.

Pitch In

As many blessings and advantages as there are to be experienced through involvement in a good church, you cannot hope to enjoy them all by just entering on Sunday mornings and experiencing the worship. Full satisfaction comes only through participation: involvement, starting to serve, lending a hand, pitching in, playing a part.

If you are a follower of Jesus Christ, you can't be a spectator, you can't just fill a seat. That is why the Bible says, "A spiritual gift was given to each of us as a means of helping the entire church."[23] God created you to make a contribution. He called you to have a positive impact on the lives of others. He shaped you in a certain way, not only for your benefit, but for the benefit of others as well.

1. *Take your SHAPE into consideration.* Rick Warren of Saddleback Church in California created a nice little acrostic for the word SHAPE that can help you think through the ways you can make a difference in your church. Warren suggested that there is a place of service for you in the church that reflects your unique SHAPE:

> Spiritual gifts—the spiritual gifts you were given,
> Heart, or passion—the things you feel strongly about,
> Abilities—musical talent, building skills, organizational skills, etc.
> Personality, and
> Experience—the things you've been through in your life.[23]

Take all those things, put them together, and you have a combination that is uniquely you; a shape that uniquely equips you for service to God. And, as mentioned earlier in this book, your church can help you discover your gifts and other characteristics and put them to work in the service of God and others (see chapter 3). But there are other factors as well.

2. *Take your church's strengths into consideration.* Your church may have a strong tradition of teaching God's Word. It may be among the best in the community at ministering to children...or seniors. Your church may operate a soup kitchen or provide crucial support to a community food pantry. Take strengths such as those into consideration when looking for a place to serve.

3. *Take your church's needs into consideration.* Many church leaders have a thrilling vision for the future, but they are praying and waiting for someone to come along to help realize that vision. You may be that

person. Ask your church leaders where the greatest needs are. Look for areas in your church that would make the biggest impact if someone—just like you— were to step in to make a difference.

Believe it or not, no matter who you are, what you think of yourself, or how little you may think you have to offer, you are very likely the missing piece of the puzzle for your church. Paul wrote to the Ephesians,

> [God] gave some to be apostles, some to be prophets, some to be evangelists, and some to be pastors and teachers, to prepare God's people for works of service, so that the body of Christ may be built up until we all reach unity in the faith and in the knowledge of the Son of God and become mature, attaining to the whole measure of the fullness of Christ.... From him the whole body, joined and held together by every supporting ligament, grows and builds itself up in love, as each part does its work.[25]

In other words, your gifts, abilities, passions, personality, and experience are absolutely crucial to the growth, maturity, and effectiveness of your church! If you are a Christ-follower, then God has given you gifts and placed you where you are so that your church can become all He wants it to be. Don't be shy. Don't feel insignificant. Don't hold back. Start serving, somewhere, in some way, and watch the pieces come together.

Reach Out

Don't panic. You don't have to knock on doors or preach on street corners. But if Jesus Christ is important to you, and if you are a part of His church, then Jesus says, "Go."[26] Share. Reach out. Tell someone. Invite someone.

Anybody can do this. You may be a one-day-old Christian, you may know next to nothing about God or the Bible, but you can still tell someone that you're going to church. You can tell them why you like it. You can invite them to come with you. You can offer to take them out to lunch after church and just talk—be human, be open, be yourself. Let them see that you're willing to share yourself and your interests—and your friends, and your Savior—with them, and you might be surprised at the results.

There are people in your world that only you can reach out to. Like you, they are people God loves. People for whom Christ died. People for whom the church exists. They're waiting for you to take a step in their direction. So take a chance. Give it a shot. You never know, they might be the next ones to read this book and discover what the church—your church—has to offer.

NOTES

INTRODUCTION
1. Genesis 1:3, ESV.
2. Genesis 1:4, 10, 12, 16, 18, 21, 25, 31.
3. Acts 1:3–5; 2:1–4, MSG.
4. Acts 2:17, 21, MSG.
5. Acts 2:28–39, MSG.

CHAPTER 1
1. Acts 2:9–11a, ESV.
2. Acts 8:14b–17, ESV.
3. Acts 10:44b–45, NLT.
4. Acts 2:7a, NLT.
5. Acts 2:12, NLT.
6. Acts 26:8, NLT.
7. Acts 4:9b, NLT.
8. Acts 8:30b, NLT.
9. Acts 14:15a, NLT.
10. Acts 16:30, NLT.
11. Acts 8:36b, ESV.
12. David Kinnaman, *You Lost Me: Why Young Christians Are Leaving Church...and Rethinking Faith* (Grand Rapids: Baker Books, 2011), 193.
13. See Acts 1:12–14.
14. See Acts 3:1–11.
15. See Acts 4:1–4.
16. See Acts 4:36–37, 6:7.
17. See Acts 5.
18. See Acts 6.
19. See Acts 6.
20. See Acts 6.
21. Romans 3:23, NLT.
22. See Matthew 6:2, 5, 16.
23. Acts 5:16, MSG.
24. Matthew 10:25a, NLT.

CHAPTER 2
1. Exodus 20:9, ESV.
2. Henry David Thoreau, *Walden: 150ᵗʰ Anniversary Illustrated*

Edition of the American Classic (Boston: Houghton Mifflin Harcourt, 2004), 6.
3. Thoreau, 3.
4. 2 Kings 6:8–23.
5. http://www.hutchcraft.com/a-word-with-you/your-hard-times/step-back-and-see-it-better-6299
6. Priscilla Owens, "We Have An Anchor," public domain.

CHAPTER 3
1. See Romans 1:19–20.
2. Matthew 28:19–20a, MSG.
3. 2 Corinthians 5:17.
4. Hebrews 10:20.
5. See Acts 3:1–10.
6. 2 Peter 3:18a, ESV.
7. C. S. Lewis, *Mere Christianity* (Gift Edition), (New York: Harper Collins Publishers, 2012), 296.
8. 2 Timothy 3:15b–17, MSG.
9. Ephesians 2:8.
10. Acts 2:21, NIV.
11. Acts 16:31, MSG.
12. Genesis 3:8, NIV.
13. Matthew 22:29, NIrV.
14. Luke 1:75, NCV.
15. 2 Timothy 3:17, MSG.

CHAPTER 4
1. William Ernest Henley, "Invictus," in *Life and Death: A Collection of Classic Poetry and Prose* (London: Icon Books, 2003), 32.
2. Genesis 2:23, NLT.
3. Ray Oldenburg, *The Great Good Place: Cafes, Coffee Shops, Book stores, Bars, Hair Salons, and Other Hangouts at the Heart of a Community* (New York: Marlowe & Company, 1989), 4.

4. Richard N. Goodwin, "The American Condition,"The New Yorker (January 28, 1974), 38.
5. Matthew 28:19–20a, MSG.
6. Romans 3:23–26a, NLT.
7. M. Craig Barnes, *The Pastor as Minor Poet: Texts and Subtexts in the Ministerial Life* (Grand Rapids: Wm. B. Eerdmans Publishing Co., 2008), 38.
8. 1 Corinthians 1:3b–7, NLT.
9. Luke 4:18–19, NLT.
10. Psalm 68:6, NIV.
11. Galatians 6:10b, ESV.
12. Galatians 6:10b, NIV.
13. Ephesians 2:19, NLT.
14. Matthew 12:46–50, NLT.
15. David Kinnaman, *You Lost Me: Why Young Christians Are Leaving the Church...and Rethinking Faith* (Grand Rapids: Baker Books, 2011), 203–206.
16. Kinnaman, 203.
17. 1 Peter 2:9, KJV.
18. Kinnaman, 203.

CHAPTER 5
1. Rick Warren, *The Purpose-Driven Life* (Grand Rapids: Zondervan Publishers, 2002), 64.
2. Acts 2:46, MSG.
3. Isaiah 6:1–10.
4. 1 Samuel 16:23.
5. Cited in G. K. Chesterton, *St. Francis of Assisi* (New York: Image Books, 1957), 78.
6. 1 Samuel 3:3, NIV.
7. Joshua 3.
8. 2 Chronicles 20:21–22, NIV.
9. Warren, 73.
10. Revelation 5:12, NIV.
11. Psalm 95:1–2, NIV.

12. Psalm 95:6, NIV.
13. 1 Samuel 13:14, NIV.
14. Psalm 5:3, NLT.
15. Psalm 63:6–7, NIV.
16. Psalm 5:7b, NLT.
17. Psalm 22:22, 25, NLT.
18. Psalm 111:1, CEV.
19. Psalm 26:8, NIV.
20. Psalm 27:4–5, NIV.
21. Psalm 20:6, NIV.
22. Revelation 4:8b, GNT.
23. Quoted by Heather Schnese, "Memorable Moments in Worship," Outreach Magazine, Sept. 10, 2011, http://www.outreach magazine.com/features/4319-Memorable-Moments-Worship.html.
24. Ibid.
25. Ibid.
26. Psalm 111:1, CEV.
27. Romans 12:1a, MSG.

CHAPTER 6
1. Annie Dillard, *Pilgrim at Tinker Creek* (New York: Harper Perennial Modern Classics, 2007), 114.
2. National Research Council and Institute of Medicine, *From Neurons to Neighborhoods: The Science of Early Childhood Development* (Washington, D.C.: National Academy Press, 2000).
3. See Move: What 1,000 Churches Revealed About Spiritual Growth by Greg Hawkins and Cally Parkinson (Grand Rapids: Zondervan Publishers, 2011).
4. Luke 11:1.
5. Acts 8:26–40.
6. 2 Timothy 1:6b–8a, NLT.

NOTES

7. 1 Peter 2:2–3a, NLT.
8. Acts 12:1–6, NIV.
9. Acts 12:7–16a, NIV.
10. Acts 12:16–17, NIV.
11. Acts 12:5, NIV.
12. Acts 12:11b, NIV.
13. Acts 12:16–17, NIV.
14. Romans 12:15, NIV.
15. Bill Hybels, *Courageous Leadership* (Grand Rapids: Zondervan Publishers, 2002), 22–23.

CHAPTER 7

1. Max Lucado, *Outlive Your Life: You Were Made to Make a Difference* (Nashville: Thomas Nelson Publishers, 2010), xix.
2. Lucado, xx–xxi.
3. Paul David Tripp, *A Quest for More: Living for Something Bigger Than You* (Greensboro, NC: New Growth Press, 2007), 14.
4. Acts 2:38–39, MSG.
5. Acts 2:41–42, MSG.
6. Hebrews 12:22, NLT.
7. Hebrews 12:22, NLT.
8. Hebrews 12:23, NLT.
9. Hebrews 12:28, NLT.
10. Daniel 2:44, NIV.
11. 1 Corinthians 12:6–11, NLT.
12. 1 Corinthians 12:12–21, NLT.
13. Dave Earley, *The 21 Most Effective Prayers of the Bible* (Uhrichsville, OH: Barbour Publishing, Inc., 2005), np.
14. Acts 2:44–45, MSG.
15. Acts 4:32–35, MSG.
16. Acts 6:1–7, NLT.
17. R. Joseph Hoffman, ed./tr., *Julian's Against the Galileans* (Amherst, NY: Prometheus Books, 2004), 156.
18. John 5:17, GNT.

CHAPTER 8

1. John Donne, Devotions Upon Emergent Occasions, Meditation XVII.
2. James 4:14, NASB.
3. Kenny Loggins, "This Is It," © Sony/ATV Music Publishing LLC, Warner/Chappell Music, Inc., Kenny Loggins—Gnossos Music and Milk Money Music, EMI Music Publishing .
4. Psalm 139:4–6, NIV.
5. Acts 13:1–3, MSG.
6. Acts 9:27a, MSG.
7. James 4:14, NASB.

CHAPTER 9

1. Anne Morrow Lindbergh, *Gift from the Sea* (New York: Pantheon Books, 1955), 115.
2. "Easing Brain Fatigue With a Walk in the Park," Gretchen Reynolds, The New York Times, March 27, 2013. http://well.blogs.nytimes.com/2013/03/27/easing-brain-fatigue-with-a-walk-in-the-park/
3. See Genesis 1–3.
4. See Revelation 21–22.
5. Romans 5:1–5.
6. Romans 5:6–8, 11–12, 14b–18, NLT.
7. John Milton, "Paradise Regained," lines 1–7.
8. Acts 9:2b, NLT.
9. Acts 9:5b, NLT.
10. Acts 9:17, NLT.
11. Acts 9:18-19, NLT.
12. Acts 9:19b, NLT.
13. Psalm 46:10.
14. Matthew 11:28, NLT.
15. Kasey Hitt, personal interview with author.

16. See Acts 9:36–41.
17. Acts 9:32–35, MSG.
18. Bobby Ross, Jr., "Addicts Find Hope, Healing Through Recovery Ministry," The Christian Chronicle, http://www.christian chronicle.org/article877~Addicts_ find_hope,_healing_through_re covery_ministry
19. Alanna Davis, "Both Small and Large Churches Offer Effective Recovery Ministries," http:// www.abbaconnect.net/both-small-and-large-churches-offer-effective-recovery-ministries/

CHAPTER 10
1. Brenda Ueland, If You Want to Write: A Book About Art, Independence, and Spirit (Nashville: BN Publishing, 2010), 9–10.
2. http://www.goodreads.com/ quotes/422467-unexpressed-emotions-will-never-die-they-are-buried-alive-and
3. Based on John 3:1–15.
4. John 3:8b, NASB.
5. Luke 6:45, NIV.
6. See Acts 8:4–40.
7. See Acts 13:46.
8. Jeanne Theoharis, The Rebellious Life of Mrs. Rosa Parks (Boston: Beacon Press, 2013), 6.
9. Exodus 31:1–11, NIV.
10. See Acts 16:11–15.
11. 1 Thessalonians 2:1–8, NIV.
12. Acts 9:27a, MSG.

CHAPTER 11
1. Acts 4:23–24a, NIV.
2. Acts 11:5, NIV.
3. Acts 12:12b, NIV.
4. Colossians 4:12, NIV.

5. Acts 4:34–37, NIV.
6. Acts 9:19b–25, NIV.
7. Acts 16:1–5, NIV.
8. Acts 20:7–12, NLT.
9. For Paul's guidelines regarding the characteristics of overseers see 1 Timothy 3.
10. Acts 20:36–38, NIV.
11. Acts 27:1–4, NIV.
12. Acts 27:3b, NIV.
13. Acts 28:11–15, NIV.

CHAPTER 12
1. Ecclesiastes 11:4, NLT (1996).
2. Joshua 3:17, NIV.
3. See Acts 9:23–25.
4. See Acts 9:23.
5. See Acts 9:26.
6. See Acts 9:28–30.
7. See Acts 6:1.
8. See Acts 15.
9. See Acts 1:14.
10. See Acts 6:7.
11. See Acts 8:26–40.
12. See Acts 9.
13. See Acts 10:1.
14. See Acts 16:11–15.
15. See Acts 17:34.
16. See Philippians 4:22.
17. John 3:3, NIV.
18. John 3:6–8, NIV.
19. John 3:14–17, NIV.
20. 2 Corinthians 5:17, NLT.
21. Galatians 3:26–27, NRSV.
22. 2 Corinthians 5:17, NLT.
23. 1 Corinthians 12:7, NLT.
24. See Erik Rees, S.H.A.P.E.: Finding and Fulfilling Your Unique Purpose for Life (Grand Rapids: Zondervan Publishers, 2008).
25. Ephesians 4:11–16, NIV.
26. Matthew 28:19; Mark 16:15, NIV.

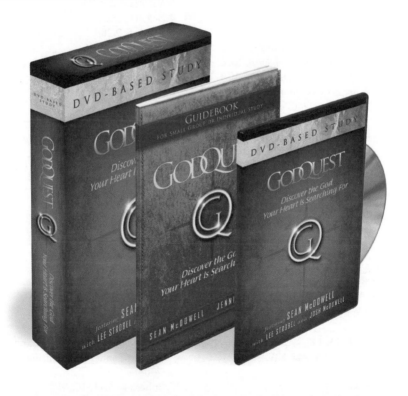

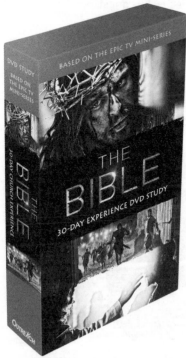